ADDICTION, CODEPENDENCE, PROCRASTINATION AND LAZINESS: A GUIDE TO UNDERSTANDING, OVERCOMING AND PREVENTING RELAPSES

Lindsey Anderson

BOOK DESCRIPTION

Addiction, codependence, and laziness are the three great impediments to personal development. This book, "Overcoming addiction, codependence, and laziness" is a resource guide aimed at helping those who are suffering from either of these impediments to overcome them and lead highly rewarding and productive lives.

Addiction is a big threat to society. We have heard of high-profile deaths due to drug addiction, more so, in celebrity circles. Unfortunately, these are just but a tip of the iceberg. Many people die because of addiction without their cases reaching the media's antenna simply because they are not VIPs. Some of them are innocent victims killed by those under the influence of drugs such as drug-influenced mass shootings. Apart from deaths, there are those living perilously wasted and ruined lives due to addiction. They can neither function normally nor productively contribute to their wellbeing and that of society at large. Some of the consequences of drug addiction could have been prevented had loved ones known their root causes and thus helped the victims avoid falling prey to drug abuse and addiction. In this book, you will not only be able to identify the types of addiction and their triggers, but also their root causes. Furthermore, you will be able to learn how to heal from addiction and lead a productive life thereafter.

Codependence is the most hidden of these three impediments to personal development. Most of the time, one party to codependence – the Taker, is often identified while the other party – Caretaker, remains muted. Yet, the Caretaker suffers as much as the Taker, if not more. Caretaking has largely been considered a 'virtuous' form of 'benevolence' and thus encouraged by a society that is mostly unaware of its negative consequences. In this book, we are going to explore what codependence is, its symptoms, likely negative consequences and how to overcome it. Codependence is just as severe as a behavioral addiction - with negative consequences that impede personal development and productivity.

Laziness is the most widely talked of these three impediments. In almost every family, someone will be touted as 'lazy'. This is in view of the low levels of productivity associated with such a person. Without leading a productive life, personal growth and development are impaired. Like addiction and codependence, we often focus on the symptoms rather than the disease. We never go beyond castigating the symptoms to find out the root causes of laziness. Thus, we end up leaving the problem largely unaddressed. Laziness affects one's education, career, employability, income potential, and livelihood. These are not things that can be treated lightly. In this book, we will discuss the root causes of laziness. We will also discuss how to overcome it so that we can lead productive lives as responsible members of society.

You can stop addiction, codependence, and laziness. All you need is the power to do so. Knowledge is power. This book is a powerful tool for you to stop addiction, codependence, and laziness. You can save yourself, relative, friend, peer, colleague or neighbor by simply applying the knowledge provided in this book.

Enjoy reading!

DISCLAIMER

CONTENTS

INTRODUCTION

Addiction, codependence, and laziness are three main perils ravaging our youths today. With these three perils, families are destroyed, economies rendered unproductive, and heritage wasted.

Though youths are the age group that is the most ravaged by this epidemic, it would be unfair to lump up the entire bulk of blame onto them. Senior adults are also suffering from this epidemic, more so alcohol and nicotine addiction. The youths just happen to be the vulnerable majority. The increasingly discreet nature of drug consumption and peddling networks means that teenagers can easily buy and take drugs without being noticed by their parents and guardians.

The best way to defend yourself or loved one against addiction or to rise from the depth of addiction is to arm yourself with adequate knowledge about it. While there is plenty of literature about drug addiction, there is hardly any literature that bundles these three perils as interdependent elements. This book explores these three impediments to personal development in a wholesome perspective with a special focus on their impact on health, wellbeing, and productivity. The book goes further to provide durable solutions to these epidemics thus helping victims overcome them, heal and lead productive lives thereafter.

Keep reading to learn more...

CHAPTER ONE: WHAT DRIVES PEOPLE INTO ADDICTION AND CODEPENDENCE

We have been so used to hearing the word 'addiction' such that it has become a norm rather than an exception. Most of the time, we look at it from the symptoms perspective rather than from the root cause perspective. Without looking at it from the root cause perspective, we are more likely going to prune the branches instead of uprooting the entire tree.

Codependence suffers much more severe fate in the sense that most people never realize that it is indeed something bad and with negative consequences. Most of the time, it is taken as something positive especially from the perspective of the Caretaker.

In this section, we are going to explore what addiction and codependence are and consider their root causes.

What it means to be addicted and codependent

The best way to understand what it means to be an addict or codependent is to know what the two are.

What is addiction?

Addiction is a condition that makes a person engage in a behavior or consumption of a substance for the sake of gaining rewarding effects that have highly compelling incentive for repetitive pursuit despite the adverse negative consequences.

What is codependency?

Codependency is a learned pattern of behaviors and beliefs that result in a relationship in which two people engage in mutually destructive habits and maladaptive coping mechanism.

Maladaptive coping mechanisms are those mechanisms that a person adopts which limits the person's normal functioning and thus diminishes life satisfaction.

The fundamental difference between addiction and codependence

Addiction is a disease, though it has habitual component. On the other hand, codependence is purely habitual. Codependence is simply a learned habit.

What drives people into addiction

There are many factors that drive people into addiction. These factors vary from one person to another. However, beyond the branches of symptoms and the fruits of consequences, there are deep underlying roots that are neither visible nor easily discernible.

Yet, without getting to the roots, trimming the branches in order to prevent flowering and fruit formation will not stop the addiction.

To have a better insight into what drives people into addiction and other matters involving addiction, we will be exploring some of the addiction cases that I have come across through many years of my practice as a consultant psychologist, specializing in the field of relationship and drug addiction.

About 20 years ago when I had just started practicing in New York, I met a man named Kevin. He was one of my first patients. He told me about his wife, whom he has been married to for 10 years. Kevin was a very responsible man when he married. However, after delivery of their second child, Kevin started getting drunk occasionally on the weekends. Nevertheless, with time, this became severe as he started drinking in the evenings during weekdays. When they delivered their last child, things turned for the worse. By the time their last child was 2 years old, Kevin was lost in the depth of alcoholism.

What makes someone like Kevin who was such a respectful and responsible man touted as the best model of a boy while growing up, and eventually a good husband and father after marriage, to turn suddenly into an addict?

Before we can get into deeper details about Kevin to identify the root cause of his addiction, let us first understand the root causes of addiction.

The root causes of addiction

There are three main root causes of addiction. It is from these three primary roots that other secondary and tertiary roots come about - mental hook, adaptation, and higher experience.

Mental hook

Mental hook refers to those factors related to the brain that pull (hook) people into addiction. In some sort of a way, they act like electric magnets that pull their victims towards addiction. A mental hook is created by either altered brain chemistry or genetic predisposition.

Altered brain chemistry can occur in two ways: pre-addiction mental alteration or post-addiction mental alteration. Pre-addiction mental alteration occurs prior to addiction. It is often triggered by mental illness such as depression. Post-addiction mental alteration occurs after addiction. It is caused by the effect of addiction, which results in a vicious triggering of more desire towards addiction. Post-addiction mental alteration is secondary in effect.

Besides Kevin, John is another one of my early clients in New York. John suffered from severe drug addiction. He was not only an alcoholic, but also a chain smoker, and womanizer (sex addict). John turned the exact opposite of his father in so many ways. Unlike John, his father (Peter), a priest was a teetotaler, monogamous and faithful to his wife.

What would make such a wonderful father to beget such a son? Well, the environment within which John was brought up was a church compound in a much more secluded place. He went to a seminary school. In his early childhood and teenage, he did not have bad friends. So, what turned him to addiction later after?

It turns out that John's grandfather (Andrew) exhibited most of his characters. In fact, he was a serious addict with a history of drug abuse (alcohol, tobacco, and marijuana), a string of women, three divorces, several rehabilitations, and relapses. Eventually, he committed suicide because of the addictions and failure to recover.

Indeed, Peter was taken up and educated by the church. He had run away from home due to his father's physical and verbal abuse and a good Samaritan introduced him to the Church, which enrolled him in a child support program that they ran.

As we can see, there is a striking resemblance between John's addiction and that of his grandfather, Andrew. While he may have engaged in other forms of addiction that were unlike his grandfather's, they were secondary in nature as part of his coping mechanism. Did genetics play a role? We shall see this later.

Adaptation

Adaptation is about using drugs as a coping mechanism. Adaptation could be due to trying to cope with:

- Extreme pain – this pain could be physical, mental, psychological or emotional.
- Phobia – this phobia could be due to fear of failing exams, fear of punishment and retribution, among others.
- Environmental constraints – hostile environment such as prison, war, harsh weather, etc can push some people into addiction in order to cope.
- Peer pressure – teenagers are the most vulnerable to peer pressure. A teenager will be pressurized to do what others in his/her group are doing to identify with them and not feel the odd one out. Grown-ups too can be susceptible to peer pressure, though they are not as vulnerable as teenagers.

What drove Kevin, a man who had manifested a high level of responsibility during his boyhood and early life as a husband and father, into an alcoholic derelict?

Well, digging further into Kevin's history, those who knew him described him as having been a very obedient, humble and polite boy. However, his father was a substance abuser (alcohol, tobacco, and cannabis). His alcoholic father used to beat him up on flimsy grounds. Sometimes Kevin's mother would also be beaten up when she tried to intervene.

Thus, although Kevin managed to survive the difficult childhood that was characterized by physical, emotional and psychological abuse, he was left with deep inner scars that no one ever realized. He was a traumatized child. The qualities that his school and the community within which he lived praised for, were simply camouflage. They hid the turmoil within. His 'good manners' during his childhood were a coping mechanism to the harsh home environment. However, when he got free from his father, the same coping mechanism could no longer work. Instead, the childhood trauma started aching him and thus he had to devise a new mechanism to cope with it – alcoholism.

Genetics

Scientists have found out that people with certain type of genetic strains are more likely to become addicts. Genetics increase the tendency for people who are already susceptible to addiction due to other factors to become addicts. It is estimated that close to half of all cases of addiction have some genetic factors. However, genetic factors on their own without other factors can remain mute and largely suppressed. In most cases, it is the non-genetic factors such as adaptation that triggers them.

By examining John and taking cognizant of his history, my colleague, a consultant neurogenetic psychiatrist, identified that John had a mental condition that made him more susceptible to substance abuse and sex addiction. Further genetic screening exposed that John had genetic traits that are commonly found in a significant population of those who are addicted. John revealed that two of his own maternal uncles were also alcoholic and one died due to it. Thus, John's case was of a genetically-derived mental hook (Pre-addiction mental alteration).

Higher experience

Wanting to have an extraordinary experience can tempt one to try out drugs and continue using it in order to retain such a higher experience. This higher experience could be the desire for boosted performance such as the desire to excel in exams, athletics contest, sexual intercourse, preaching, public speaking, acting, and singing, among others. It could also be the desire for ecstasy such as desire to feel good, especially during parties and celebrations.

More often than not, the desire for higher experience is the cause of multiple addictions. For example, there are many people who smoke cigarettes or marijuana only when they are drunk. When they are sober, they never abuse these other substances.

One patient who I treated after he became and addict as a result of desire for higher experience was Edgar. Edgar always endeavored to 'conquer' women. He always desired to exhibit the traits of a macho man. He spent a lot of time in the gym just to build up his muscles. When not in the gym doing muscle building, he would be in the salon trying to boost his appearance. He was always concerned about his appearance. He always wanted to seduce women and have them his way.

His desire to 'conquer' women made him become a sex addict. Every time he desired a higher sexual experience than before. To boost this sexual experience, he became so eager to boost his male organ and libido. This pushed him into taking libido-enhancing drugs – a kind of stimulants.

It would seem obvious that Edgar was seeking higher experience. However, a keen look at his background reveals some deep underlying root causes. While Edgar had a responsible father in his early childhood, the father, later, became an addict by the time he turned age 7. When his father turned into an alcoholic, he used to insult him as to how he is irresponsible and lazy. By the time he became a teenager, his father was already an absentee father, just coming home occasionally after a long while.

Due to the father's absence, Edgar relied on the care and upbringing of his mother and elder sister. In some sort of a way, he grew up being 'soft' and thus used to be teased and bullied by others, more so ladies, for being 'a sissy'. This made him develop the excessive consciousness of wanting to prove that he is a man after he became an adult. Was his sex addiction a desire to subdue women? Well, it could be.

Multiple roots

Just as an individual may suffer from several addictions, it is also possible that the root causes could be several. There could be a primary root begetting secondary roots.

I have dealt with patients with multiple root causes of addiction. One such typical patient was Maria. Maria was the third and last born of her parents. Maria was largely conscious of her appearance. This drove her addiction to cosmetics, skin lighteners, fashions and the like. Even though she was a beautiful young girl, that never stopped her from being overly conscious of her appearance and not feeling satisfied with it.

Maria was largely taken care of by her elder sister as her largely 'single' mother went out to look for money to take care of her family. The father was an alcoholic and eventually started abusing other hard drugs. He was largely absent coming home just occasionally, providing nothing except a financial burden and a source of violence and abuse.

Her mother had the financial burden of taking care of the family, despite not having good education and skills to provide her with a stable employment that could guarantee her some reasonable income. This meant that Maria could not receive sufficient stipends from her mother to support her cosmetics addiction.

What made her be so conscious about her appearance and turn her to cosmetics addiction?

It may seem that her consciousness and desire to look beautiful made her become a cosmetics addict. However, this is more of a symptom rather than the root cause. Maria's father used to abuse her while drunk. He often scolded her by uttering, "You fat ugly lazy bitch! You are just as ugly as your mother."

Maria also had a problem with acne and obesity. She was also plumb. To add on that she was dark-skinned as her mother. Her father was White while the mother was African-American. Her father's insults appeared racist in nature – the kind of negative views his friends engendered. To make it worse, her father never insulted her elder sister who was light-skinned. This made Maria feel ugly and unwanted, just for being dark-skinned.

A largely absentee father whose occasional appearance seems to have been just to come and insult her and torture her family made her have a poor foundation in her relationship with men. By the time she was in her mid-teenage, she had started seeing multiple men. In one sense, she was seeking her dad in men, as the men she was seeing were not within her age bracket but much older. Another secondary factor was the desire to finance her addiction. Since the men gave her money for cosmetics, she found it kind of a symbiotic relationship. Although, the downside of it is that some misused her and left her more desperate, more longing and more clinging. This desperation pushed her into marijuana addiction. She suffered from low self-esteem. To enliven her moments so as to be charming to her new male targets, Maria found taking Marijuana to be her best option. However, the embrace-reject kind of relationships created violent emotional swings, which pushed her to take Ketamine as a relief.

Looking at it, Maria suffered from multiple root causes – childhood trauma (father's abuses and absenteeism), and desire to feel high.

Key elements of Addiction

Knowing the key elements of addiction can help in breaking the entrapment of its vicious cycle. The following are the key elements of addiction:

- Reward – there is actual or perceived gain.
- Motivation – there is compelling incentive to continue the pursuit of the reward.
- Reinforcement – there is a repetitive action that allows reinforcement of the habit.

- Memory – there is a memory of the past reward, which acts to incentivize repetition.

- Impaired control – Every reinforcement wears down one's willpower and hence inability to control the addiction.

- Compulsion – with impaired control, engaging in addiction becomes almost automated.

- Negative consequences – the addiction brings forth negative mental, psychological, emotional, physical, social and/or economic consequences.

What drives people into codependence

Unlike addiction, codependence is one of those challenges that most people never realize exist. This is because those who suffer from codependence (especially the Caretakers) sometimes exhibit likable characters that are commonly touted as great virtues and when they manifest some other not-so-pleasant traits, it is considered normal human imperfections. As such, Caretakers are mostly encouraged by unknowing members of the family and society.

Like drug addiction, codependence has its own reasons. The following are some of the common reasons that make one become a codependent (Caretaker):

- Wanting to please

- Wanting to avoid conflicts
- Fear of loneliness
- Fear of being rejected
- Being unable to properly handle challenges of emotional intimacy
- Being overly concerned about other people's affairs and feelings such as to take them as personal responsibility
- Having the natural tendency towards being a caregiver
- Not being able to handle negative criticism

The root cause of codependency

Like an addiction, codependency has its root causes. Codependency is a pain in adulthood whose roots emanate from childhood trauma and acts as a coping mechanism. It has a high tendency of lead to relationship challenges and addictive behaviors.

The relationship between codependence and addiction

Addiction and codependence are two dangerous partners. An addict has a high potential of attracting a codependent and vice versa. A codependent (Caretaker) will have an overwhelming sense of obligation towards 'saving' and 'uplifting' an addict. On the other hand, an addict will feel attracted to a codependent since the addict feels that a codependent 'understands' the addict's situation. In this case, the addict will be the Taker.

Furthermore, codependency is usually accompanied by behavioral addiction. On the other hand, both addiction and codependence can be triggered by the same source.

CHAPTER TWO: ADDICTION TYPES

Being able to know addiction types will enable you to identify the type of addiction you or your loved one suffers from and handle it appropriately. Some addictions are so obvious such that you know when you or your loved one is becoming an addict. However there are addictions that are more difficult to detect unless you are informed. The hardest part is detecting someone else's addiction, more so, teenagers. Teenagers present a real detection challenge to parents and caregivers as they discreetly engage in addictive behaviors due to restrictions already imposed on them. They learn to go around restrictions in hideous ways.

There are many types of addictions. However, they can be classified into either substance addiction, or behavioral addiction.

Substance addiction

Substance addiction is a progressive relapsing condition resulting from compulsive substance use despite one's knowledge of its negative consequences. This condition impairs user's ability to control or quit the substance being abused.

Substance addiction is made possible by two critical factors – tolerance and dependence.

Tolerance occurs when the body tolerates a certain given quantity of the same quality of substance such that the user will require an increasingly higher consumption of the same quality to achieve the same level of effect.

Dependence occurs when the user has to consume a given substance in order to feel 'normal'. When the user fails to consume the substance or consumes in quantities that are not above tolerance level, withdrawal symptoms appear which makes the user feel 'abnormal'. This sense of 'abnormality' forces the user to take the substance in quantities above tolerance level in order to get back to 'normalcy'.

Addictive substances

There are many types of addictive substances. These addictive substances can be classified into five main categories - stimulants, hallucinogens, depressants, opioids, and dissociatives.

Stimulants addiction

Stimulants are a type of drugs that alter the functioning of the central nervous system thus causing the user to feel hyperactive. This hyperactivity is characterized by an increase in heart rate, increase in blood pressure, higher breathing rates, and increased blood sugar levels. These cause higher levels of alertness.

Some stimulants are prescribed by doctors to remedy asthma, narcolepsy, and ADHD. Stimulants can be consumed in many forms, which include drinking (e.g. caffeine), huffing (e.g. cocaine), among others.

Popular types of stimulants include Caffeine, Synthetic marijuana, Ecstasy, Ritalin, Methamphetamine, and Adderall, among others.

Edgar is one patient who used several stimulants including caffeine, ecstasy, and methamphetamine. He took them with the aim of boosting his libido so as to advance his sexual performance.

Hallucinogens addiction

Hallucinogens derive their name from the effect of their consumption – hallucination. Hallucinogens disrupt normal communication within the brain system thus causing non-existent perceptions such as the appearance of ghosts. Users also experience highly intense and rapid shifts in emotions.

Hallucinogens can be consumed in many different forms. These include ingestion (as pills, tincture, food, or beverages), and smoking, among other ways. Popular types of hallucinogens include Psilocybin, Peyote, LSD, and Salvia.

Depressants addiction

Depressants are normally prescribed for purposes of relieving anxiety, obsessive-compulsive disorder, insomnia and other medical conditions that render the victim restless. They are sedative by nature.

Those who abuse depressants aim to avoid stressful situations. Depressants can be consumed in form of pills or drinks. Popular types of depressants include Barbiturates, Valium, Rohypnol, Benzodiazepines, and Xanax.

At later stages of Kevin's addiction, he started using valium. He felt this was helpful for relieving his stress.

Opioids addiction

Opioids are a special type of powerful painkillers that induce a sense of euphoria when consumed. They are usually prescribed to patients suffering from extreme pain. They are a product of the poppy plant.

Opioids can be consumed in many different forms. These include ingestion (e.g. pills, tincture, and beverages), injection, and smoking, among other ways. Opioids are highly addictive. One can become addicted after just 3 days of regular consumption. Popular types of opioids include Opium, Morphine, Heroin, Vicodin, Hydrocodone, Codeine, Oxycontin, and Percocet.

Doreen was one of my few clients who suffered from codependency (we shall discuss her case later under codependency). She did not deliberately seek to abuse drugs. But, as a result of her pain due to years of hard chores and bodily neglect, she received various medical prescriptions to suppress her deep pains, mostly due to arthritis. However, she tended to overdose and even take when she was not feeling pain just to prevent likely onset of pain – especially at night.

Doreen is a typical case where effects of codependency unexpectedly pushed her to drug addiction.

Dissociatives addiction

Dissociatives are drugs that make users feel as if they are external observers to themselves. They feel as if they are no longer part of their body and as such, the body belongs to someone else. In essence, the users dissociate themselves from their own being. Dissociates disorients users' sense of reality which makes them have some sort of an invincibility and allows them to engage in risky behaviors such as robbery, violence, extreme activities, among others.

Dissociatives work on the brain by interfering with its glutamate chemical receptors that are significantly responsible for pain perception, cognition, and emotions. Dissociatives can be consumed in all substance forms including gas, liquid, solid, or powder.

Popular types of dissociatives include Phencyclidine (PCP), Dextromethorphan (DXM), and Ketamine.

Cannabis addiction

Cannabis has been the most controversial drug. The controversy surrounding cannabis dates back to over 700 years ago. However, whether its usage is legalized or not, just like any other drug, it has serious consequences when severely abused. Various global statistics indicate that Marijuana (cannabis) is the third most widely used recreational drug after alcohol and tobacco.

Marijuana has both hallucinogenic and depressant properties. When it comes to consumption, Marijuana is the most versatile drug. It can be ingested (as pills, tincture, food, or beverages), smoked, sniffed, injected, among other ways.

Kevin, Edgar, and Maria abused Marijuana. In all the cases, it was due to peer influence. However, Maria never smoked marijuana. Instead, she took the tincture of marijuana as she was allergic to many types of fumes.

Inhalants addiction

Inhalants are a broad category of drugs that only share one thing – they are gaseous fumes, some of which can cause euphoria. Users get addicted to them, either out of the need to feel euphoric (gain higher experience) or out of the need to relieve discomfort e.g. asthma, flue, allergy, etc (as part of adaptation).

The most commonly abused inhalants are nitrous oxide, room deodorizers, aerosol sprays, and fumes of glue, paint, paint thinner, gasoline, and markers, among others. This is the most common form of addiction by street children in poor developing countries.

Nicotine (tobacco) abuse

Tobacco is both a stimulant and a depressant. Tobacco addiction is the most fatal of all addictions in terms of the sheer number of victims it sends to the grave every year. It is estimated that tobacco causes over 5 million deaths annually. Nicotine is the main compound in tobacco that causes addiction. Nicotine is a highly addictive and psychoactive compound.

Kevin and Edgar abused tobacco. Though, unlike Kevin who was a chain smoker, Edgar smoked tobacco on an occasional basis, especially while drinking with friends as a way to get high.

Alcohol addiction

Alcohol is a depressant. Although one may initially experience a rapid upsurge in energy, this capsizes quickly in just a few minutes.

Though Edgar and Maria took alcohol occasionally, they were never alcohol addicts. However, Kevin was a severe alcohol addict.

Behavioral Addictions

Behavioral addiction is an addiction that involves compulsive desire to engage in non-drug-related rewarding activities despite the negative consequences to the person's mental, emotional, psychological, physical, social and/or economic well-being.

Common symptoms of behavioral addiction are:

- Consistent preoccupation with the addictive behavior
- Impaired ability to control the addictive behavior
- Increased tolerance to addictive behavior
- Becoming dependent on the addictive behavior as a means of coping with emotional disturbances
- Sacrificing productive activities such as work, education, family, etc because of behavioral addiction
- Hiding or minimizing the extent of your behavioral addiction
- Adverse withdrawal symptoms when resisting or avoiding the behavior
- Detrimental psychological withdrawal symptoms such as anxiety or depression when resisting or avoiding the behavior

Extreme symptoms of behavioral addiction:

- Doing or saying harmful things because of the addictive behavior
- Harming loved ones because of the addictive behavior
- Losing valuables or compromising health or relationship due to addictive behavior

The main categories of behavioral addictions are food addictions, recreational addictions, relationship addictions, digital addictions, shopping addictions, work addictions, exercise addictions, and cosmetic addictions, among others.

Food addictions

Food addiction is one of those addictions that most people never realize that they are suffering from unless they are alerted. Many people never think about stopping food addiction as they consider it harmless. Yet, not all food addictions are harmless. Some of them are extremely severe and manifest dangerous withdrawal symptom just as hard drugs.

The main types of food addiction are sugar addiction, caffeine addiction, and bingeing.

Maria was a food addict, more so, a sugar addict. She had craving for sweet things.

Recreational (Leisure) addictions

While recreational activities are great for passing free time, socializing, refreshing and even regeneration, some of them can have the opposite effect when they become addictive.

The main types of recreational addiction that I have encountered are gambling addiction, sex addiction, and porn addiction.

Edgar was both a porn and sex addict. He liked reading and watching porn content. He had a constant desire to engage in sex and was always eager to have sex with almost every other woman that his eyes could land on.

Relationship addictions

It is natural to think about relationships as mutual, consensual and beneficial to both parties. However, the reality can be different. There are those who end up losing willpower in a relationship while others carry the burden of it on behalf of their uncommitted partners.

The most common types of relationship addiction are clinging, obsessions, and love addiction.

Maria had a love addiction. Maria had a string of multiple relationships, which were triggered by an inner desire of wanting to feel loved. The fear of ceasing to be loved by a man made her have multiple relationships as some form of security. Though she obtained material benefits out of it, it could be compared to a daughter longing for and wanting material cover from her father. The father was largely absent in her childhood and thus she seemed to unconsciously seek her father's love from other men.

Digital addictions

It is no doubt that we are in a digitized world. We can hardly fathom how to live without electronic gadgets – computers, smartphones, tablets, TV sets, calculators, gaming devices, etc. In one way or another, we are using a digital gadget in our life.

We have become so reliant on digital systems such that some of them have made us addicts. If for any reason you find yourself cursing, feeling irritated, moody, angered, etc, because you cannot watch a movie, visit social media, or play a video game, then know that you are either a digital addict or gradually falling into the traps of digital addiction.

The most common types of digital addictions are internet addiction, social media addiction, and video games addiction.

Shopping addiction

Shopping addiction happens when you tend to buy things that you desire but not necessarily need. Shopping addiction can occur in two forms – either impulsive buying or sentimental buying. Impulsive buying occurs when you buy something on the spot just by seeing it without having prior plan or aforethought about it. On the other hand, unlike impulse buying, sentimental buying occurs when you buy based on emotional tendencies. For example, buying items just because seeing them brings back some memories is a form of sentimental buying. You do not necessarily need to buy but you are buying out of some sense of nostalgia. The same happens when buying jewelry, souvenirs, and expensive timepieces.

Work addiction

Work addiction is a common disease among career persons. Work addiction occurs whereby you fail to demarcate between working hours and non-working hours such that you compulsively continue working beyond working hours. There are those who sleep at workplaces, not necessarily because the work is urgent, but because they find it hard to leave their workstations.

Exercise addiction

Exercise addiction is a compulsive tendency to carry out fitness workout such that your other normal activities are compromised. You continue fitness workouts even when you have sustained an injury and you are in pain. This is a common addiction among bodybuilders.

Edgar was addicted to exercises as a way of covering up for his sense of inferiority. He felt not man enough and the way to appear so was through muscle building workouts. He suffered from obsessive-compulsive muscle dysmorphia, also known as bigorexia.

Cosmetic addiction

Cosmetic addiction occurs whereby you unnecessarily and incessantly apply cosmetics even though further use only serves to spoil your skin, image, and overall outlook.

The common types of cosmetic addictions are skin bleaching addiction, tattoo addiction, and plastic surgery addiction.

Maria was addicted to skin bleaching and plastic surgery. This was driven by a desperate sense of feeling not being beautiful enough. She was never satisfied with her looks and thus was constantly seeking to change her looks.

The compound nature of addiction

It is common that one form of addiction can lead to another form of addiction. For example, Kevin's alcohol addiction led to tobacco, marijuana and valium addiction. Edgar's sexual addiction led to fitness addiction and stimulants addiction. Maria's cosmetic, food, and love addictions seem to have been parallel and thus none triggered the other. Doreen became an opioid addict. However, her addiction was due to abuse of medical prescription that was recommended to her to take care of her arthritis and aches due to extreme working (a consequence of codependence).

It is very rare for a person to have only one form of addiction, especially when it comes to substance addiction. Most addicts have multiple forms of addiction. It is common to find some drug addicts becoming behavioral addicts as well. This means that when it comes to recovery, the therapist must identify them and seek to know whether they emanate from the same primary cause as in case of Kevin and Edgar or multiple primary causes as in the case of Maria.

CHAPTER THREE: ADDICTION TRIGGERS

Triggers play a critical role in enforcing addictive habits. Triggers lead to cravings and urge. A trigger is simply a cue that beckons a thought, feeling or action to consume an addictive substance or engage in addictive behavior. There are two main types of triggers - internal triggers and external triggers.

Internal triggers

These are triggers, which originates from within oneself. They can be thoughts, feelings or memories that become sensitized and hence bring forth urges and cravings. The three main types of internal triggers are emotions, physical sensations, and attitudes.

Emotions

Emotions are by far the commonest of all addictive triggers. Some of the common emotions that can trigger one's addictive tendencies include phobia, anxiety, loneliness, self-pity, resentment, anger, indifference, boredom, fatigue, frustration, stress, depression, and other negative feelings that one subconsciously endeavors to avoid.

Kevin suffered from almost all of these triggers - most notably self-pity, anger, resentment, stress, frustration, and (later on) depression. Maria suffered from loneliness (absence of fatherly figure in her childhood), and some level of anxiety (being over-conscious of her appearance).

Phobia and anxiety

Phobia is an irrational and dilapidating fear characterized by extreme anxiety that severely interferes with quality of life or ability to function normally.

Phobia is characterized by two critical components: catastrophic thoughts, and evasive behavior. Catastrophic thoughts are thoughts about something bad happening. On the other hand, evasive behavior is characterized by taking action to avoid an occurrence of the perceived catastrophe.

It is common to find people who have certain phobia resorting to drinking or taking marijuana in order to gain confidence to deal with their phobias.

Some of the common phobias associated with addiction include:

- Social phobia (fear of public interactions) – this can make one seek substance abuse in order to feel comfortable in social places.
- Enochlophobia (fear of crowds) – this may aggravate emotional and social triggers.

- Glossophobia (fear of public speaking) – this may cause one to seek substance abuse in order to gain the confidence of addressing the public.
- Agliophobia (fear of pain)- this may trigger abuse of opioids.
- Aviophobia (fear of flying) – this may aggravate emotional triggers.
- Monophobia (fear of being alone) – this may cause anger, resentment, self-pity, clinging, and obsession.

Physical sensations

Physical sensations can trigger addictive tendencies, more so if they are associated with what you seek to remedy by consuming a given substance or engaging in a certain addictive behavior. The common types of physical sensations include pain, fatigue, panic, hunger, sexual arousal, and senses (smells, tastes, sounds, touch, sight, etc)

Doreen became addicted to opioid prescription due to extreme pain. Edgar experienced abnormal sexual arousal largely due to his defective mindset (attitude towards women).

External triggers

External triggers are those that originate outside oneself. The two main types of external triggers are environmental triggers, and social triggers.

Environmental triggers

Environmental triggers are those cues within your surroundings that bring about memories, feelings, and thoughts of addictive tendencies. The three main types of environmental triggers are places, things, and situations.

Places

If you have a habit of engaging in addictive substance or behavior at a certain place, then visiting or being in that place will trigger the addictive tendencies.

High-risk places that can trigger addictive tendencies include bars and clubs (alcohol and smoking); hotels, restaurants and fast-food places (food addiction); lodgings, brothels and massage parlors (sex addiction); friend's home (cracking); worksites (work addiction); bathrooms (cracking, masturbation); former drug-stash locations (cracking); shopping malls (shopping addiction); salons (cosmetic addiction); gyms (exercise addiction); casinos (gambling addiction); and cybercafés (digital addiction), among others.

Things

There certain things that we often use while consuming addictive substances or carrying out addictive behaviors. Seeing these things will trigger addictive tendencies.

High-risk things that can trigger addictive tendencies include magazines (pornography addiction, sex addiction, food addiction, etc); furniture (e.g. bed for sex addiction); cash, credit cards/ATMs (shopping addiction); empty pill bottles / unattended pills (drug addiction); television/movies (digital addiction, pornography addiction, sex addiction, food addiction, etc); wine/spirit bottle (alcohol addiction), and bong (marijuana addiction), among others.

Pornographic materials (magazines, moves, etc) often acted as triggers for Edgar's sexual addiction.

Situations

Situations and events can trigger addictive tendencies more so if one tends to engage in addictive activities during such situations/events.

Common situations/events that can trigger addictive tendencies include emotionally charged interactions (e.g. upsetting news, political arguments, and criticism); holidays, celebrations, or sporting events (e.g. anniversaries, graduations, winnings); time-based events (e.g. breakfast - coffee, break time -junkie snacks, lunch and dinner time -bingeing, weekends - alcohol, Christmas season -bingeing, alcoholism, and cold season - coffee), among others.

CHAPTER FOUR: THE ROAD TO RECOVERY FROM ADDICTION

Addiction is one of the shortest roads to perdition. It is when a person arrives at the junction of realization that this road is destined to hell that the person finds the need to change course towards the road to recovery.

Like every journey, the road to recovery has stages. There are five main stages on this road to recovery, each with its own onerous tasks and milestones to be achieved - Pre-contemplation, Contemplation, Preparation, Action, and Maintenance.

Pre-Contemplation

Pre-contemplation is a stage in the darkness. It is when you are still deep in addiction; yet, the consequences of addiction are hitting hard to wake you up. It is when light is still seeking you in the dark, yet, like a thief, you keep on running away from it.

This light could be the law enforcement officers finding you on the wrong side of the law and giving you a last warning, or that important person in your life who discovers the secret of addiction that you have kept for so long and advises you to quit. It could also be a serious injury that you incur due to addiction such as breaking a limb or collapsing unconscious due to overdose and finding yourself awake in the ICU. Other than harming yourself, it could be about harming someone else such as a severe injury that you have inflicted on your loved one or neighbor because of your rage due to the influence of substance abuse.

This light comes in many forms. You may run away from one or buy time, but eventually, an incessant light will incessantly shine on you and you realize that things cannot continue the way they are. You realize that you can no longer continue to be a resident in the darkness. You realize that it is time to become an enlightened citizen of this world.

While you keep on hiding from the light, you keep on blaming other beings, things or circumstances for your inability to turn around. You keep on seeking justification as to why the darkness is the most appropriate thing for you. But, this road is always short – though, at times it can be fatal.

Kevin had gone through violent encounters due to his addiction. He engaged in bar brawls with fellow drunkards. One day he slid on the staircase and broke his arm. It took the effort of his wife to attend to his medical needs.

He felt a sense of guilt seeing his wife and family spending the toils of their hard work on him while he contributed nothing financially to the family. This prompted the thoughts of him giving up his alcoholism, yet, he still recovered from the injury and went back to alcoholism.

There are several times he got arrested for misdemeanors due to the influence of alcohol but he still could not give up taking alcohol.

He fell into a ditch and broke his leg. Just as he had broken his arm, it was again his wife and family to take care of his medical needs. This time around, he stopped taking alcohol for a while; yet, relapsed later on.

Contemplation (Awareness, Realization, and Acknowledgement)

Like every other thief, a light eventually shines on you such that you are left with no reason to seek darkness any more. Your cover of darkness has been the addiction. It has kept you in some sort of safety away from the responsibility of being who you ought to be. Eventually, you realize that it can keep you no more. You can no longer find excuses to continue being under its cover. It is at this moment that you start contemplating salvaging yourself, liberating your mind and setting yourself free.

At the contemplation stage, you become aware of your nakedness. You see it. You realize that it is not the best for you. You want to be dressed and addressed like others. Reflections come where you visualize yourself being free. However, you are still overwhelmed by the cost that comes with it – the cost of responsibility.

There is both the sense of anxiety and excitement. The anxiety of what it will be when you step out of this cover. How you are going to confront the demons of darkness that have held you hostage for such long. How costly it is going to be in terms of rebuilding yourself.

Excitement comes when you realize that there is great potential for overcoming your addiction. You foresee greater benefits that come with overcoming addiction. The benefits look greater than the cost you continue to incur as an addict plus the cost you have to incur to end your addiction.

There will be interludes of hope and despair, faith and disbelief. Nevertheless, like water flowing into a can of oil, the more the water (good will) continues to flow into the container (willpower), the more the oil (bad will) continues to flow out in displacement.

What broke the camel's back in Kevin's case was the near-fatal accident he encountered. He had borrowed a friend's car and used it for some days. However, one day he decided to drive himself to his usual drinking dens. He misinterpreted the amount of alcohol he had already consumed and felt he was still sober enough to drive himself home. Unfortunately for him he had a terrible accident.

He could not remember what happened but he woke up in a hospital ward. The eyewitnesses said that he veered off the road and hit a giant billboard pole. The vehicle was wrecked, and he sustained serious life-threatening injuries.

It is at this juncture that Kevin got convinced that he had to accept help in recovery from his addiction. Furthermore, as part of sentencing for dangerous driving, he was convicted to communal service. In addition to that, he had either to agree to a voluntary supervised rehab or be forcefully detained in an involuntary rehab camp. Yet, despite the sentencing, Kevin had made up his mind that he had dangerously veered off from life and the next point was probably death. What if instead of a pole it was a human being? He could not fathom the consequences of hitting someone to death. The damage he had caused his family, his own being and now his friend woke him up. He had not renewed his driving license. He could not even renew it because he had been prohibited from driving for having been caught several times driving under the influence of alcohol. This meant that the insurance company could not compensate the car since it was being driven by an unauthorized person under the influence of alcohol. More debts to pay due to his alcoholism – a burden left to the wife and family.

Preparation (exploring recovery)

Once the water of faith and hope displaces the thick oily slug of addiction, you start preparing yourself to have a new clean beginning. You decide that it is time to put your contemplation into a plan of action. You start preparing yourself for rehabilitation. This is a mental work rather than physical work.

At this stage, you have taken the bold step of seeking information from those who can help you recover. You have probably visited a rehabilitation center and gotten details of their programs and schedules. You are preparing yourself on how to attend and honor your commitment.

Kevin visited rehabilitation center on his first appointment, which was more of familiarization with his rehabilitation center and to acquire more information about what he needed to do. It is at this moment that he met me and formally became my client.

Action (Consideration)

Every journey begins in the mind. Before you take the ignition keys to drive your car, the journey already started in your mind. The pre-contemplation, contemplation and preparation steps are done right within you. The action is about stepping out to work – work on your recovery plan.

It is at the action stage that the addicts open up to being assisted to free themselves from the yokes of addiction. This assistance could include clinical rehabilitation experts depending on whether the addiction is of substance or behavior - and its severity. It is not always that rehabilitation experts are called in. However, unlike with most behavioral addiction cases, most substance addiction cases require the intervention of rehabilitation experts. This is primarily due to the strong mental hook that cannot be removed without consideration of the serious damage. In addition, vital organs could have been compromised or weakened - such that they have become too dependent on the coping mechanism to drugs. Hence, instant withdrawal could mean instant collapse. This was the case of Kevin. Some of his internal organs had been severely compromised.

The positive thing about intervention by external parties is that the addicts feel wanted, cared for, and their situation being understood. This gives them the motivation to take bold steps into their recovery effort. The action stage has the three key processes - evaluation, stabilization, and transition.

Evaluation

This is the first process in the action stage. It is where experts carry out tests, screening, and assessment to determine the extent of the damage that addiction has inflicted on the patient.

It is upon the evaluation of the extent of the damage that the experts can be able to ascertain the type and nature of intervention based on the ability and strength of the body to withstand the intervention.

Stabilization

Stabilization is about taking measures, which ensures that the body remains stable and functional during the withdrawal.

In most cases, victims of substance abuse suffer from malnutrition due to neglecting diet. This means that their bodies are extremely weak to withstand the effects of withdrawal. In such cases, the experts will have to prescribe or administer special diet in order to fight the malnutrition so that the body will be strong enough to withstand withdrawal and the medication required to deal with addiction including healing damage, cleansing the body off the addictive toxins and regeneration.

It is also at the stabilization stage that the patients are taught about expectations such as withdrawal symptoms, what to do about the symptoms, how to conduct themselves, and what to avoid as they undergo recovery process and the likely side effects of the medication.

Transition

Transition is a stage where one starts to deliberately depart from the vicious cycle of addiction and take a straight way to recovery. It is at a point where one takes the straight direction after the roundabout.

The transition stage has several phases, which include withdrawal (abstinence), early recovery, honeymoon, the wall, and adjustment.

Withdrawal is the initial phase after stabilization. It is at this phase when one withdraws from the use of a substance. Thus, the body is engaged in the process of getting rid of accumulated toxins due to addiction. Since the body has been accustomed to accommodating the toxins and adjusted itself to tolerate the toxins, withdrawal means that the body is undergoing painful process rewiring itself and healing. It is like removing objects, which the roots have entangled themselves on. If the process is sudden, the roots may be injured or become too exposed to the scorching effects of the strong rays (of sudden recovery mechanism). This means that the process has to be monitored and managed such that the pace is not too fast as to injure the body.

Depending on the severity of withdrawal symptoms, the patient may be admitted so that close monitoring and management is done.

Early recovery is the next phase after withdrawal. The body gradually starts to overcome the effects of addiction and rebuild. You no longer feel the adverse effects of withdrawal.

Honeymoon comes when one starts consolidating the positive gains after addiction. The person feels neither the urge nor reminiscent thoughts to fall back to addiction. The person looks forward to much bigger gains beyond addiction. The person is ready to settle down. It is like one's marriage with desired future, which marks the departure from the solitude of addiction. However, just like divorce occurs after marriage, it is important for the person not to become overly confident to the point of ignoring the need to nurture this new marriage.

At this stage, there is a high wall to be climbed. One has to muster enough muscle to climb it over into the future, failure to which one will have to turn back. It is at this stage when reflections in the past come, memories of the past outpour, and cravings knock. One may feel suspended and overwhelmed by a sense of desperation as to why things are not changing as quickly as they anticipated.

The wall epitomizes a point of breaking off from the past. Like with every honeymoon, at some point midway, partners start thinking about children, building a home, having sustainable earnings for the family and many other obligations and responsibilities. Sometimes the obligations and responsibilities may look scary. It is also time to reflect on the cost so far incurred during the 'wedding', its preparations and the honeymoon. If the bridegroom took heavy loans in order to have the wedding and classic honeymoon, he would be counting on the cost and feeling the heat of fire ahead. The former addict is the bridegroom in this case. This may look scary and thus put a strain on the newfound relationship and the future dreams and vision.

Adjustment happens after one has successfully jumped over the wall. At this phase, the person is adjusting to realities of settling in life. This happens about four months after the wall. The person is more focused on the future and excited about it. There is no motivation to look back. However, this does not mean that one has completely buried the past. The scars of addiction are still visible. What makes the big difference is the consolidation of a positive attitude after a change in mindset. There is still rebuilding effort. The home is still taking shape. New additions are still taking place.

Maintenance

At this stage, the focus is to maintain the sober state. The effort is towards maintaining healthy habits and goals that the person on recovery set up to achieve during the initial stages of recovery. It is at this stage that one becomes involved as an active participant in sobriety activities. Joining groups such as Narcotics Anonymous, or Alcoholics Anonymous and others relevant to the kind of addiction one suffered from is important. This way, there is the reinforcement of sobriety that comes out of those who are at the maintenance stage supporting one another. The main aim is the keep the sobriety status long enough to create a wide, high and permanent barrier to relapse.

Dealing with the consequences of addiction

Addiction has consequences. Some of the consequences are reversible while others are irreversible and even fatal. It is important to know the consequences of addiction and be able to deal with them. Otherwise, without appreciating the damage already done, then, there is a higher likelihood of failure to completely recover or even relapsing after recovery. The consequences of addiction not only afflict oneself but also family, loved ones, and colleagues.

CHAPTER FIVE: PREVENTING RELAPSE

Recovery is a great leap away from addiction. However, it is not an assurance that there will be no receding. The best way to build a barrier against sliding back is to prevent relapses.

Every moment you relapse your resolve become weakened as your willpower get worn out. Thus, preventing relapse is extremely important, no matter the cost.

To be able to prevent relapse, the first and foremost step is to understand its common causes so that you can avoid them.

Common causes of addiction relapse

To know the common causes of addiction relapse is the best way to get prepared to fight relapse. The following are the common causes of addiction relapse:

1. Persistent exposure to triggers

We have already discussed addiction triggers before. Triggers are the ones that reinforce the vicious cycle of addiction. Thus, you must avoid knowingly exposing yourself to them.

2. Persistent craving

Craving is because of a trigger. The trigger does not have to be physical. It can be mental, emotional, hormonal, or even circumstantial. When cravings set in, they are raising the mental flag.

3. Stress

Stress works to tire your resolve thus making you more susceptible to triggers and cravings. Stress can be physical, mental, emotional, social or psychological. When you feel stressed, identify the source of stress and stay away from it.

4. Overconfidence

Overconfidence in any endeavor often yields sub-optimal results. It causes you to bite more than you can chew and at times make assumptions and ignore warnings. This is more likely going to result in stress when you fail to achieve your targets.

5. Self-pity

It is almost certain that when you reflect to your life prior to addiction and on the present relative to others, you are likely going to feel self-pity since addiction either has retarded your progress or swayed you from your long-term goals. The best way to avoid self-pity is to build an engaging relationship and be active so that you do not have the time and sorrowful conditions that can result in self-pity. You must also avoid the disease of comparison. Do not fall into the trap of comparing yourself with others who progressed while you regressed under addiction. Comparing yourself to others is the surest way to engender and nurture self-pity.

6. Dishonesty

The worst thing is to be dishonest to yourself. Addiction is always accompanied by dishonesty. This could be dishonesty to others but mostly dishonesty to yourself. You are mostly denying the negative consequences and loss of control until it becomes extreme. Similarly, after recovery, the very same dishonesty that drove you to addiction may cause a relapse. The best way to avoid dishonesty is to be transparent, disciplined and accountable. Whenever there is an urge or craving, talk to those who are responsible for helping you in your recovery process so that they can help you come up with a solution. They could find a way to keeping you company, joyful and occupied.

7. Unrealistic expectations

Those who have been addicts for a long time are like newly released prisoners after a long sentence. They always feel that there are immense opportunities available to them after redemption. They have already received positive words of encouragement, which have raised their level of expectations. However, it is important to be realistic. You will need to sharpen your skills, find a job, restart or re-ignite your relationships that were either neglected or died when addiction became too much for them to withstand.

You need to set up realistic expectations. The best thing to do this is to have post-recovery goals, objectives, and milestones. Set them to be in tandem with your pace. This way, you will be happy achieving them step-by-step. Let your loved ones, mentors and sponsors participate in setting your goals, objectives, and milestones. They can always act as your independent observers and can let you know that although you had properly set the goal, it was too big to achieve within that particular setup. This will let you know that you did your best and thus you never failed.

8. High expectations of others

During the recovery process, you are highly likely to receive a lot of support. This support will start to fizzle out gradually as you advance in your recovery. This is natural and a good thing. If this support does not gradually decline, you will not learn to become independent and chart your own path. Instead, you will move away from the ditch of addiction and fall into the ditch of codependence.

Thus, it is important to know that there comes a time when others get back to focusing on their own affairs as you focus on your own. Do not get frustrated that you are no longer receiving the attention and support that you used to receive during the recovery period.

9. Boredom

Boredom is lack of creativity. It is a way your mind tells you to find something creative to do. If you fail to find and engage in something creative, the mind might trigger some craving as a way of preoccupying you. Thus, whenever you start feeling bored, find something creative and engaging to preoccupy your mind.

Going outdoors, taking your pet for a walk, going to swim, participating in sports activity or community charity service, are some of the ways by which you can kill boredom. One important thing is that you must overcome the inertia that keeps you stuck away from engaging in creative activities. Boredom is evidence that your mind is stuck and needs to be pushed to keep rolling – of course, in the right direction.

10. Phobia

Quite a number of addictions are due to phobia. Thus, it is important to address the phobia that pushed you into addiction. Find ways to overcome it. Share your concerns with those who are supporting you so that they can provide a mechanism by which you can address and overcome your phobia. This may require the expertise of a professional psychologist.

11. Relationship crisis

Relationship crisis can easily cause stress and depression, which can result in addiction triggers. If there are those relationships whose frustrations pushed you into addiction, end them. If a new relationship is not working, end it. Yet, do remember to guard yourself against another serious enemy – loneliness.

12. Undiagnosed mental health problem

A significant number of addicts have mental problems as the deep underlying root cause. Sometimes what could be a symptom could be misdiagnosed as a root cause. For example, phobia, stress, anger, and anxiety can be because of mental illness. This means that they are symptoms rather than the disease. Thus, without proper diagnosis, this disease will not be healed and thus the victim is likely going to relapse.

Unfortunately, most patients suffering from mental illness will not detect that they are suffering from it. It requires a professional expert such as a psychologist or psychiatrist to discover that the person is suffering from mental illness.

13. Loss of control

Those people who become addicts because of emotional instability are the ones who are more susceptible to losing control. For example, people who abuse drugs because of anger are easily going to relapse when they become irritated and lose control of their anger.

14. Loss of judgment

Loss of judgment is often because of loss of control. If you are angered and unable to control it, you are more likely to take actions not based on sound judgment. This could result in relapse as you lose the better judgment that would otherwise dissuade you from relapsing.

Common triggers of substance abuse relapse

We have identified triggers are the as one of the most common causes of relapse. Let us look at some of the common triggers of relapse (as opposed to addiction). The following are the common triggers of relapse:

- Severe negative emotions – the most common of these emotions are the H.A.L.T emotions. H.A.L.T is an acronym for hungry, angry, lonely, and tired. You have to stop the H.A.L.T. whenever it sets in.
- Artifacts – artifacts are those things that symbolize addiction. Most of them are the tools that you used in consuming addictive substances (e.g. bong, rollers, beer bottles, etc) or engage in addictive behaviors (e.g. sex dolls, sex toys, porn materials, etc, in case of sex addiction).
- Places – these could be places where you used to procure your substances, consume your substances or engage in

addictive behavior. They could be bars, brothels, lodgings, etc.

- People – these could be those people you used to abuse substances with or those you used to engage addictive behavior with. They could also be people who used to provoke you into anger or cause you to have a phobia.

- Isolation and loneliness – these are conditions that allow you to reflect on your past and revise your past memory of addiction.

- Relationships – if you became an addict due to relationship crisis, then, re-engaging the same relationship is more likely to trigger relapse if the crisis repeats itself.

- Lack of proper self-care – failure to engage in active leisure activity, live in a dirty or cluttered environment, eat a poor diet, deny yourself enough quality sleep, among others, are examples of poor self-care. They are more likely to trigger stress and anxiety.

- Withdrawal symptoms – most people relapse during the recovery stage because they are unable to cope or endure severe withdrawal symptoms. Such symptoms include weakness (e.g. fatigue, shaking, etc), anxiety, nausea, among others.

- Post-acute withdrawal symptoms – these are extreme and abnormal withdrawal symptoms. They may be due to the severe effect of substance abuse or recovery mismanagement. Such symptoms include violent mood swings, extreme anxiety, dilapidating physical weakness, and extreme nausea, among others.

Edgar recovered from addiction and showed greater signs of improvement. However, the death of his father took a heavy toll on his life. He became indignant, stressed, and in some sort of a way felt remotely responsible for his father's death as he was never around to care during his long period of sickness.

Luckily, he encountered a lot of support from family and friends who were motivated by the desire to not allow him give up on life since he was the only one in the family with the potential to step into his father's shoes in helping the family. The death of his father became the rallying point for family and friends not to give up on him.

Maria recovered from her addiction. The father's confessions and asking for forgiveness the way he treated her had a great impact on her. This provided the impetus for her to break the vicious cycle of seeking 'her' father in the older men she dated. They became close friends, and this helped her cope with the post-recovery scenario.

The stages of relapse

Relapse is not an event but a process. To be able to effectively prevent relapse, you have to understand the process of relapse by knowing its stages. The three crucial stages of relapse are emotional relapse, mental relapse, and physical relapse.

Emotional relapse

Emotional relapse is one of the earliest stages of relapse. It is characterized by setting up your emotions towards possible relapse in future. This is evidenced by emotional behaviors such as mood swings, intolerance, anger, anxiety, isolation, defensiveness, avoiding help, evading meetings (post-recovery group meetings), poor eating habits (due to loss of appetite), and erratic sleep patterns.

These are characteristic of symptoms encountered during post-acute withdrawal. To be able to prevent total relapse, you must deal with emotional relapses as soon as possible, as it is much easier to reverse than later stages when the relapse has deepened its roots into your psyche.

Emotional relapse prevention

The best way to prevent slipping deeper into emotional relapse is to recognize your emotional relapse behaviors and change them. For example, if you realize that you are drawing yourself into isolation, seek the help of others. Join groups, clubs and community organizations. More importantly, participate actively in the post-recovery group.

When it comes to anger, anxiety, intolerance and mood swings, the best way to deal with them is to practice mindfulness meditation and exercises such as yoga.

Poor eating and sleeping habits can be overcome by deliberately practicing self-care. Make sure that you eat a balanced diet based on regular meal schedule. When it comes to sleeping, avoid distractions during sleeping hours and make sure that you go to bed on time and wake up on time. This way, you will not distort your sleeping patterns.

Mental Relapse

In mental relapse, your mind is pre-occupied with ideas about taking the drug. You are actively debating whether to take or not. There is push and pull between these two primary thoughts. You are trying to rationalize the temptations of relapse.

The signs of mental relapse are:

- Fantasizing about using drugs or engaging in addictive behavior
- Thinking about things, places, and people in relation to your past addiction
- Getting comfortable with and accepting the addictive actions and behaviors of your old friends

- Glamorizing your past addiction experiences
- Thinking about relapsing
- Actively planning your relapse
- Lying about your thoughts when asked about by those in charge of your recovery
- You become overwhelmed in resisting the urge to relapse

How to deal with mental urges

The best way to dealing with mental urges is to distract them. Whenever the urge comes, try to overcome it by doing something else that pre-occupies your mind such as playing a game, taking a walk, turning on inspiring music or simply calling a friend.

However, distractions are temporary measures. The long-term measure is practicing mindfulness.

Physical Relapse

Physical relapse is the last stage of relapse. It is where you actually indulge in the addictive substance or behavior. You may choose to take alcohol, opioids, marijuana, tobacco, or cocaine. This is an extreme stage where reversal becomes increasingly difficult.

The dangers of relapse

Relapse has a very negative impact. It is like a truck that recedes while on a steep hill. It means that more effort will be required to stop the recession, and much more will be required to move it forward again, not forgetting that the distance lost during recession must be recovered. The worst is a relapse in substance abuse.

The following are some of the negative effects of relapse:

- **Body wreck** – In substance abuse, when you are at the stage of recovery, the body adjusts its tolerance level in its healing effort. Thus, when you relapse, the body is found in a much vulnerable position than it was before you started the recovery process. This may cause severe damage to the organs including lungs (for tobacco smokers), liver (for alcoholics), brain (for severe substance abusers), and skin (for both alcoholics and tobacco smokers), among others. Your body's defense mechanism suddenly goes down which makes you more susceptible to infections, disease, and illness. On the other hand, lower tolerance level means that taking a dose that you used to take before recovery process began is most likely going to result in an overdose. This could be fatal depending on the substances that you are abusing.

- **Psychological damage** – when you relapse, your self-esteem becomes injured. This means that it becomes harder for you to get back to the recovery process and even sail through successfully. Having experienced sobriety after withdrawal, relapse means that you are more likely to regret, feel guilty and become more emotionally hurt. You will most likely want to take more dosage just to overcome your sense of guilt thus spiraling further into the vicious cycle of substance abuse.

- **Broken bonds** – while in the recovery process, there will be people who will have dedicated themselves to helping you get through. When you relapse, you lose their trust and faith. Some will give up and a few will probably hold on, albeit, faint-heartedly. This is the bond that one would not wish to break.

How to overcome relapse tendencies

There are occasions when you will encounter strong urge to relapse. You must not surrender to the urges and cravings. This is when you have to be bold and disciplined.

You can overcome relapse tendencies by strengthening your willpower, being self-aware, accepting your symptoms as normal and inevitable, being positive and proactive, completing your therapy, being patient, engaging in active leisure activities, having sufficient rest, relaxation and sleep, keeping off relapse triggers, and enrolling with addiction self-help group.

How Addiction Self-Help Group works

Most communities have Addiction SHG (Self-Help-Groups). This is because addiction has become a modern disease that afflicts many. Joining addiction SHG is voluntary. It is the best way to find the support you require not to relapse. If there is no such group, do take the initiative to form one with those whom you know are also undergoing the recovery journey as you are.

It is always motivating when you hear the stories of addiction survivors because they have had the kind of experience you are going through. They will understand you much better than those who have never been addicts in their lives. They can easily detect telling signs that all is not well with you and grant you the necessary support so that you do not relapse.

The following are advantages of Addiction SHG:

Peer support – in the Addiction SHG, you will meet people who are going through the same recovery process as you are. This will help you feel not alone and odd one out. You can be able to engage each other in dialogue and feel confident that just as they are on the right path, you too have chosen the right path.

Increased self-esteem – within the Addiction SHG, you hear stories of those who have gone through your journey and made a successful recovery. This motivates you and builds your confidence that no matter how much pain your withdrawal is, you are going to be a winner. This builds your self-esteem as you can see possibilities ahead.

Opportunity for peer-to-peer learning – every group of people will always naturally find ways to teach each other lessons. Everyone goes through some instances of self-discovery. The Addiction SHG allows you to share your self-discovery techniques with others and they too share their own self-discovery with you. In the end, everyone acquires new techniques of dealing with various recovery challenges.

Freedom from judgment – it is common when you are an addict to be judged harshly by those who are not. However, when you are in the company of fellow addicts who are in the recovery process, you understand one other, and you are also together due to being victims of similar circumstances. Thus, no one feels inclined to judge another one harshly. Instead, there is more understanding of one another and a sense of deeper appreciation for being together on this journey to recovery.

An opportunity to learn different consequences of addiction – The impact of addiction varies from one addict to another depending on the degree of addiction, personal vulnerability, circumstances, and environment. Yet, having an opportunity to attend recovery sessions simply means you have probably avoided encountering some of the negative consequences that would have probably been ahead of you. Thus, learning from others about their consequences helps you to know the dangers you are likely to encounter should you relapse. More so, hearing from those who have relapsed and come back will help you note how severe the consequences of relapse are. This can motivate you to overcome the temptations to relapse.

A community to belong – Addiction SHGs are community in themselves. You are able to create a network of those who are in similar situation as you are. You have someone to go to when you feel that you are getting overwhelmed, more so, feeling lonely. Loneliness is one of those conditions that can easily trigger a relapse.

How to Get the Most Out of Your Group

Belonging to Addiction SHG is great, but not enough. How you conduct yourself within the group will determine whether you get the most out of it or not. You can get the most out of Addiction SHG by being active in the group, being committed to the group, attending group meetings regularly, and taking advantage of help being offered to you by others.

CHAPTER SIX: IDENTIFYING CODEPENDENCE RELATIONSHIPS

As we found out earlier in our book, codependence is one of the hardest things to identify. Those who suffer from codependence never realize it. The society mostly treats codependence as a virtue rather than a vice on one party (Caretaker) and laziness on the other party (Taker).

Codependent Parties

Just like in any other kind of relationships, there are two parties to a codependency relationship - the Taker, and the Caretaker.

The Taker is that person in a relationship who seeks to be taken care of. The person is always looking to receive something from the relationship. As such, the taker exhibits almost opposite characters to the caretaker.

The Caretaker is that person in a codependent relationship who seeks to nurture, to care, to offer help, to save and to see that the other person (taker) feels okay.

Cynthia was the firstborn of the family. She was a very responsible girl who assisted her mother with domestic chores. While her mother went out to work, occasionally coming late in the night after her night shift, Cynthia took care of her younger siblings. She was hardly 10 years old when she started taking up her mother's adult responsibilities.

After some time, Cynthia started doing some work for pay on a part-time basis in her mid-teens. She used to give part of her pay to her two younger siblings. Despite her mum's warnings, she would secretly give them some money.

As she reached her mid-twenties while her siblings were in mid and late teenage years, they could not match her sense of responsibility. She still did their laundry, cooked food for them, washed dishes and even made their beds. They were often lazy and preferred being idle. Despite her mother's frequent warnings and indignations, she never stopped. She harbored some sense of guilt for the rather warm treatment she received from her parents and the rather cold treatment her siblings received from the absence of both parents in their everyday lives.

Codependence patterns

To understand Cynthia's case and other codependence cases, we need to look at codependence pattern in order to identify which pattern manifests in her case.

Patterns and characteristics of codependence

The following are patterns and characteristics of codependence that can help parties carry out self-evaluation as to whether they are victims of codependence or not. In addition, those who would like to help their loved ones can use these patterns and characteristics to identify those who are suffering from codependence and help them recover and heal.

There are four main types of codependence patterns - denial patterns, low self-esteem patterns, compliance patterns, control patterns, and avoidance patterns.

Denial Patterns

As the name suggests, this pattern exhibits a sense of one's denial of being a codependent.

The following are some of the common patterns:

- Mask their painful experience through humor, isolation, hunger, etc
- Feel that they do not require others to take care of themselves
- Lack sense of empathy towards others' needs and feelings
- Fail to realize that those whom they desire to get attracted to hardly exist

- Confused feelings such that they cannot pin down their exact feelings
- Quick to label others with their negative traits and often express aggression and negativity in discreet and passive ways
- Seek to obstruct expression of their true feelings. As such they alter, mute or deny how they truly feel
- Perceive and attempt to manifest compassionate sense of altruism towards others

Low Self-esteem Patterns

Low self-esteem is a common trait for those who suffer from codependence. The following are the low self-esteem patterns:

- Endeavor to engage in activities that have the potential of getting praised and recognized
- Ever desire to look good in the eyes of others which may cause them to lie just to achieve that
- Feel embarrassed when endowed with gifts, praise, and recognition
- Find it hard to identify what they need and even more difficult to ask for it once they find out
- Have a false sense of superiority
- Subconsciously seek safety and security in others

- Find it hard to establish healthy boundaries and reasonable priorities
- Find it hard to make concrete decisions
- Look up to others as having superior behaviors, thoughts, and feelings than their own
- Find it hard to admit even the simple, obvious mistakes
- Do not consider themselves worthy of love and affection. They feel they are not worthy of it.
- Have trouble sticking to their goals, achieving their plans, and completing their projects

Compliance Patterns

Compliance is a sense of wanting to belong. It is expressed through seeking uniformity rather than diversity.

The codependents exhibit the following compliance patterns:

- Quick to make decisions without weighing their consequences
- Ready to sacrifice truth for the sake of approval from others
- Sacrifice their interests for the benefit of serving other people's interests
- Ready to offer sexual favors in exchange for love
- Shy away from expressing their worldview, opinions, feelings, and beliefs when they realize that they do conflict with those of others

- Easy to compromise their own integrity and values just to have a sense of belonging with the aim of avoiding rejection or reprimand
- Value loyalty over their rights and are ready to sacrifice their rights and interests and even endure pain just to prove their loyalty
- Hypersensitive to the feelings of others and put them as a priority over their own feelings

Control Patterns

Control patterns are often associated with caretakers. They use them to advance their control over the takers. However, takers too exhibit some control patterns. The following are some of the control patterns:

- Advance favors and gifts on those they seek to influence
- Deploy their charismatic prowess and charm offensive to persuade their would-be Takers of their compassion
- Offer pretense of agreement when it comes to conflict so as to achieve their interests
- Hold the conviction that people are incapable of taking care of themselves
- Demand that their needs be met on a priority basis

- Become resentful and agitated when others fail to honor their advice or advances for help
- Use technical or colloquial language to control and manipulate others
- Express authority and indifference or bursts of rage in order manipulate and sway outcomes into their favor
- Only accept relationship when they feel needed and have the upper hand
- Refuse to negotiate, cooperate or compromise in situations where they seem to have the upper hand or where they can assert control
- Deploy shame and blame tactics in order to exploit vulnerable emotions
- Offer unsolicited direction or advice
- Seek to sway the way others feel, think or act so as to align with their own preferences

Avoidance Patterns

Avoidance patterns are often used in situations where codependents want to avoid outcomes that do not suit their desires. The following are some of the avoidance patterns:

- Avoid expression of emotions by considering them as a sign of weakness or opening up to vulnerability

- Use language that is evasive or does not point to a dispute or a point that may trigger conflict or confrontation
- Pull people to the desired interaction but when they get closer, push them away
- Abstain from sexual, physical or emotional intimacy as a way of keeping a safe distance
- Avoid expression of gratitude
- Express harsh judgment on others' thoughts, feelings or deeds
- Deliberately act in ways that seek expression of anger, shame, and rejection from others
- Cling to positions that allow grandstanding so as not to submit to superior powers
- Subtly avoid preventing people from addictions to things, places, and behaviors that distract them from enjoying intimacy in relationships
- Refusal to employ recovery mechanisms which impairs their capacity to have healthy relationships

Note: The above patterns include those of the Takers and Caretakers.

Codependence patterns in Doreen's case

Throughout our narration of Doreen's case, the following patterns become apparent:

Denial Patterns;

- Perceive and attempt to manifest compassionate sense of altruism towards others

Low Self-esteem Patterns;

- Find it hard to establish healthy boundaries and reasonable priorities
- Look up to others as having superior behaviors, thoughts, and feelings than their own
- Subconsciously seek safety and security in others

Compliance Patterns;

- Sacrifice own interests for the benefit of serving other people's interests
- Easy to compromise own integrity and values just to have a sense of belonging with the aim of avoiding rejection or reprimand
- Value loyalty over their rights and are ready to sacrifice their rights and interests and even endure pain just to prove their loyalty
- Hypersensitive to the feelings of others and put them as a priority over their own feelings

Control Patterns;

- Deploy charismatic prowess and charm offensive to persuade her would-be Takers of her compassion
- Offer pretense of agreement when it comes to conflicts so as to achieve own interests
- Hold the conviction that people are incapable of taking care of themselves

Avoidance Patterns;

- Subtly avoid preventing people from addictions to things, places, and behaviors that distract them from enjoying intimacy in relationships

Codependence patterns in Cynthia's case

The following codependence patterns can be detected from Cynthia's case:

Denial Patterns;

- Perceive and attempt to manifest compassionate sense of altruism towards others

Low Self-esteem Patterns;

- Find it hard to establish healthy boundaries and reasonable priorities
- Subconsciously seek safety and security in others

Compliance Patterns;

- Sacrifice own interests for the benefit of serving other people's interests
- Easy to compromise own integrity and values just to have a sense of belonging with the aim of avoiding rejection or reprimand
- Value loyalty over one's own rights and are ready to sacrifice own rights and interests and even endure pain just to prove their loyalty
- Hypersensitive to the feelings of others and put them as a priority over their own feelings

Control Patterns;

- Advance favors and gifts on those they seek to influence
- Deploy charismatic prowess and charm offensive to persuade would-be Takers of their compassion
- Offer pretense of agreement when it comes to conflict so as to achieve their interests
- Hold the conviction that people are incapable of taking care of themselves

Avoidance Patterns:

- Subtly avoid preventing people from addictions to things, places, and behaviors that distract them from enjoying intimacy in relationships

Codependence patterns in Kevin's case

It may not seem apparent that Kevin was a codependent due to the common misconception that only Caregivers are codependent while Takers are not. However, codependence is a partnership and must have two or more parties to it, albeit, in opposite polarity – the Caretaker and the Taker(s).

Denial Patterns;

- Feel that they do not require others to take care of themselves
- They lack a sense of empathy towards others' needs and feelings
- They are quick to label others with their negative traits and often express aggression and negativity in discreet and passive ways

Low Self-esteem Patterns;

- Feel embarrassed when endowed with gifts, praise, and recognition
- Find it hard identify what they need and even more difficult to ask for it once they find out
- Find it hard to admit even the simple, obvious mistakes
- They do not consider themselves worthy of love and affection.
- Experience difficulty sticking to their goals, achieving their plans, and completing their projects

Control Patterns;

- Become resentful and agitated when others fail to honor their advice or advances for help
- Express authority and indifference or bursts of rage in order manipulate and sway outcomes into their favor
- Only accept relationship when they feel needed and have the upper hand
- Refuse to negotiate, cooperate or compromise in situations where they seem to have the upper hand or where they can assert control
- Deploy shame and blame tactics in order to exploit vulnerable emotions

Avoidance Patterns:

- Refusal to employ recovery mechanisms which impairs the capacity to have healthy relationships

Edgar's and Maria's cases

Both Edgar and Maria were Takers, though on a light scale. Theirs were rather normal acts of younger siblings rather an acute codependence. However, their laziness cannot be overlooked.

How to find out if you are codependent

At times, self-diagnosis becomes handy, especially when other people do not recognize you are codependent. On the other hand, some of them could be unknowing partners to your codependency.

Questionnaire to help you diagnose if you are suffering from codependence

1. Have you ever lived with someone with drug or alcohol problem?
2. Have you ever lived with someone who frequently expresses negative sentiments about you?
3. Do you find it discomforting to express your true feelings to others?
4. Do you find it troublesome seeking help?

5. Do you find it difficult to adjust to changes at home or work?

6. Do you frequently feel exasperated in the desire to find help?

7. Do you doubt your ability to be what you want to be?

8. Do you frequently feel inadequate of your being?

9. Do you find yourself being confused about your being and mission in life?

10. Do you face so many things in your life that you feel overwhelmed in terms of addressing them in a just and fair manner?

11. Do you prefer being silent just to avoid an argument?

12. Do you always get overworked about what others think of you?

13. Do you always condemn yourself when you make a mistake?

14. Do you find it difficult to turn down any request for help even though you are not in a position to comfortably offer help?

15. Do you find it difficult to accept gifts or compliments?

16. Do you feel deeply humiliated and somehow responsible when your loved one makes a mistake?

17. Do you find it difficult relating to people in authority?

18. Do you always feel like your loved one or associate could fall if you stop providing constant support?

19. Do you feel rejected when your loved ones spend time with others?

20. Do you always take other people's opinions to be superior to your own?

If your answer is yes to most of these questions, then you are most likely suffering from codependence and you need to seek professional help.

CHAPTER SEVEN: BREAKING FREE OF CODEPENDENCE RELATIONSHIPS

Codependence and addiction are very similar in terms of recovery – the journey begins in the mind. It is when parties to codependence realize its harmful effect on each other that they become aware of the need to break it. More often than not, it takes the intervention of an independent third party to intervene and help them realize their suffering and its consequences.

While it is easy to detect addiction, it is not so straightforward to detect codependence. On the other hand, while it takes unlearning to break free from the learned behavior of codependence, it takes rehabilitation (whether self or through the third party) to recover from addiction. Severe substance addiction may require medical intervention. However, codependence does not require medical intervention.

As we have seen earlier, Doreen never realized that she was in a codependence situation. This is primarily because she learned that early in her life. It was more of an adaptation scenario. She had to adapt to the racial environment that existed at the time and made worse by the domestic situation. She was more of a victim of the system. However, when she got married, surprisingly, Gerald (her husband) sensed this act of codependence from her side (as a caregiver). Although, Gerald felt that she was just a victim of the racist system who needed to be helped to unlearn from it, he never realized at that time that he too was codependent. He did not realize that it was his codependence tendencies (as a Taker) that attracted Doreen to him. It is when Gerald stopped being a responsible husband and thus ending up depending on Doreen for financial support that it became evident that he was a codependent.

Unfortunately, for Doreen, it took a heavy toll on her to realize the severity of her situation. Spending a whole day doing menial jobs and standing for long hours resulted in a severe backache, which drove her into taking opioids. Things took a worse twist when arthritis set in which meant heavy dose. Yet, it also meant that she would not attend to her menial jobs as she used to. She also became hypertensive. All these helped to consign her on her journey to the grave.

The unhealthy situation that Doreen found herself in was due to overworking and neglect. She was reluctant to seek medical attention until it was already late. Her body largely became derelict. The last stroke hit her when she was discovered to have an advanced tumor in the breast. Had she sought attention early, this could have been addressed.

The last moments of her life, on her deathbed, the family got together to be with her before her soul departed. It was a rare encounter for the entire family. It is at this moment that her husband, Gerald, realized he had neglected her and had he intervened early, she would have broken her vicious cycle of codependence. I attended this meeting by the bedside. It is a moment when many confessions came up. It is at this moment when the family realized that Doreen's mission on earth was folding up and she would not be there for them to depend on. This became a wake-up moment for them.

How to break away from codependence

Breaking away from codependence is about learning, resetting your mindset and unwinding yourself from the entanglement of old habits that perpetuates codependence.

The following are the steps you need to take in order to break free from codependence:

1. Learn more about codependency

Knowledge is power. The more you learn about codependence the more you become empowered to deal with it. This book is one such source of knowledge. However, you need to supplement it with other sources of knowledge such libraries, rehab centers, and lectures on codependence. You can also consult experts such as therapists within your locality who can help you identify some of your destructive behavioral patterns and thus learn how to overcome them.

2. Look to Your Past

Like in Doreen's case, your childhood past is the key to discovering the hidden root causes of your codependency. Equipped with the knowledge about codependency, make an audit of your own childhood past:

- Audit your family history
- Find out if there was an emotional abuse or neglect
- Seek to identify events in your childhood past that caused you to decouple yourself from your true feelings and thus ignoring your own emotional needs

Sometimes, this can be a difficult process. It could lead to pain, shame, anger, sadness or even guilt. Yet, without going through this process, it will not be possible to uproot the causes of your codependence. Practicing mindfulness can be a great way by which you can be able to deal with your thoughts, feelings, perceptions, behaviors, and both mental and physical processes without judgment that often breeds resentment, anger, pain, shame, guilt, and sadness. Without judgment, there is no pain and suffering. Note that at this juncture you are the doctor and not the patient. Take that posture of you being the doctor treating a vulnerable patient – your delicate inner being.

3. Recognize Denial

A lot of times, those in codependence relationships deny the fact that they are codependents. This is because of the scary consequences of feeling helpless with no apparent solution in sight. However, without overcoming self-denial, the healing process cannot begin. You must be honest and admit that the relationship is dysfunctional. Recognize the problem and only then can a solution become feasible.

4. Visualize your Ideal World

The best way to marshal the willpower to get out of codependence is to visualize the ideal world where you are a free and independent person. By visualizing your ideal world, you will be able to set goals to snap out of the nasty trap of codependence that you are in.

5. Detach and Disentangle Yourself

Disentangling yourself from the web of codependence requires that you detach from those beings and things that bind you into codependence. You are a system on your own relating to another system on its own. It is through synergy that these two systems become subsystems of a larger system – partnership. However, it is always necessary for you and your partner to have some degree of independence so that both of you can optimally function for the greater good of the partnership. Should the attachment threaten this optimality, then, decoupling and detachment become inevitable for the survival of a healthy partnership.

Decoupling can take the form of simple things such as financial independence, separate bank accounts, separate projects, etc. Working to please your partner is unhealthy coupling. It causes unhealthy attachment, which yields codependence. A partnership is not about one sacrificing his/her own system so that the other's system can flourish. It is about the mutual sacrifice of some independence for the mutual benefit of the whole partnership. Otherwise, if one sacrifices for the partnership to lose optimality, then, it is a dangerous sacrifice with negative consequences to both parties and the entire partnership.

6. Learn Independence

Learning independence requires effort and determination. It is like that of a toddler learning to stand up (freeing the buttocks) and walk (freeing the knees) from dependence on the ground. From a toddler, you will learn that it is not the giant steps that matter most, but the small, trembling, unstable steps that matter most. Do not shy away from slides and falls. A toddler does not, why should you? You have to learn to create moments to be alone and do things on your own.

Find new interesting hobbies to engage in. Learn to shop on your own, go to the gym alone, go to the movies alone and just enjoy your time alone. In this case, 'alone' does not necessarily mean without someone else but without the person whom you are in a codependent relationship.

Independence also means switching roles. Make arrangements such that there is a schedule to interchange performance of routine work. This way, your partner can experience what you do and by that reflect on how it affects you. This can greatly change your partner's attitude and thus contribute to avoiding codependence.

7. Establish personal boundaries

Like the way independent countries have clearly demarcated boundaries, you too should have clearly demarcated boundaries. This should be established very early in a relationship, more so, prior to deep engagement. You have to establish 'red lines' and protect them with zeal and vigor. Avoid compromises that result in you erasing your boundaries while others encroach into your territory. You will end up becoming colonized. Avoid psychological manipulations that make you become a perpetual victim. You have no capability to control what others do as that is right within their territory. But, you can control your response and reactions that overflow to your territory. Yet still, you have a right to stop encroachment into your territory.

Marking your demarcations clear and bold will make others be aware when they are encroaching your territory and the consequences thereof. This way, they will be able to know the importance of keeping boundaries in order to have good 'neighbourly' relationships.

8. Create your own positive space

Create and guard your private space. Let your own aura fill it. People in codependent relationships often neglect their private space by either leaving it and joining others' private space or inviting others to camp into their own private space.

Preoccupying yourself with other people's actions and thoughts and feeling responsible for them is one such symptom of not having your own positive private space. Your private space is not just physical but also mental, emotional, psychological and spiritual.

Letting other people's actions and thoughts to preoccupy your mind is to cede your private mental space to them. It is immaterial of whether you are physically alone or not. You also need private emotional space. Yeah, sometimes it is better to cry alone in your private space than cry on the shoulders of a codependent. It is not always that emotional space must become a sub-domain of social space. It is good to share emotions but not in a way that you cede your emotional space.

Quietude and solitude are great spiritual virtues of self-reflection. There are volumes of books that talk about the great benefits of meditation. Meditation is simply a technique that allows you to own your spiritual space. Practice meditation more often and you will start experiencing yourself being in high spirit. This is important for self-motivation and self-esteem.

9. Take breaks from each other

We have talked about decoupling, disengaging, detaching, and disentangling yourself. You can only achieve these if you are independent. Without independence, this will be a big struggle, for you must attain independence first for you to be able to exercise these options.

Taking a break from each other is the best way to allow proper ventilation into your relationship. Your relationship needs fresh air to freely flow. Being excessively entangled in each other's space will bring boredom and resentment. Doing things on your own or with friends will also allow your partner to take the same cue. This way, you will come back to each other more refreshed and with a newer perspective on each other and your relationship as a whole.

10.   Practice Self-care

Self-care is a product of self-compassion. Self-compassion is about showing love to your own being. It is about understanding and appreciating your being and its strengths and weaknesses. It about caring for your being. Neglecting your being is lack of self-compassion. Not accepting your weaknesses and taking the blame for mistakes not of your own making is lack of self-compassion.

Self-compassion is about being kinder to yourself. It is about treating yourself as you would treat your friends and loved ones who are suffering or need your care. Learn to avoid aggressive self-criticism, negative self-talk, and negative beliefs about your self-worth.

To become self-compassionate, start becoming aware of your needs, feelings, and thoughts. Find ways of communicating the same in your relationship. Make yourself understood. Do not shy away from expressing them in whatever decisions, acts or conducts that your partner makes.

Beyond the mental, psychological, and emotional self-care, you too need to make sure that you undertake social and physical self-care. Do not sacrifice your social wellbeing for the sake of your partner or partnership. This will help neither. Take care of your social relationships as the exterior partnership to your interior partnership.

Physical self-care includes having a proper diet, exercising regularly, having sufficient rest and relaxation, and attending medical checkups.

Above all, keep a journal of what goes on in your life. This way, you can be able to examine your needs, wants, values, thoughts, and opinions. This will make you not be overwhelmed by other people's opinions of you or subjugating your own opinions to their favor.

11. Learn to Say No!

The power of 'NO!' is by far the greatest power you can ever possess. Slavery is a result of the inability to say No! This is the power that resides deep within you and whose switch no one else except you have access to it. Obviously, there are those situations where you may need to avoid loudly expressing a straight No if doing so saves you from imminent danger. However, what matters more is whether you have expressed it internally or not. Remember, being forced into conditions of slavery does not make you a slave. What makes you a slave is when you accept it internally by saying Yes to it. If you cannot shout no externally due to threats to your life, you must not forget to shout it internally. This has a strong effect on your mind and attitude.

12. Learn to speak the truth

One of the strengths of being able to say No and mean it is being able to speak the truth. The 'yes' person hardly speaks the truth. A 'yes' person lies about true feelings like smiling when they ought to frown, showing joy when they ought to show indignation. They would rather suppress their true feelings than express them freely for fear of hurting others in their relationship.

13. Don't be a people-pleaser

The aim of 'yes' person is to please. This is one of the most overt signs of codependence. Almost all Caretakers in a codependence relationship are the 'yes' kind of persons. They would rather hide the truth about their true feelings and dislikes about what their partner is doing. They will get hurt and cover-up their wounds just for others to feel comfortable and satisfied.

A lot of times, the 'yes' persons seek to manipulate their relationships by offering goodies such as offering free things, doing extra favors when they ought not to. Thus, they are not innocent victims but manipulative victims of their very own circumstances. They do all these in the hope of avoiding conflict, receiving accolades, being liked, getting praises and attention for their generosity while internally they are suffering and bleeding.

To break free from codependence, exercise free will. Make choices that energize you and advance your free mind. You may be hurt in a short-while for saying No, but in the long-run, you will be freer and happier.

14. Focus on your preferences

It is important to consider your likes and dislikes. Keep those likes and dislikes that help you to be a better you by enhancing a great relationship with your inner being. Learn to embrace those things that make you happy and avoid those that make you unhappy. Weigh these in terms of two compassions – self-compassion and compassion for others. Compassion for others does not necessarily mean doing things that please them nor does self-compassion only mean doing those things that please you.

Your likes should be towards attracting greater good and not selfishness. Yet still, your dislikes should be about repelling harm and not embracing pride. Compassion helps you to distinguish between good 'likes' and bad 'dislikes'. This is where wisdom plays a greater part. It is not just about surrendering to the primitive instincts but weighing them out.

15. Don't be a slavish martyr

Martyrdom is dying for the interest of others. While genuine martyrdom is about compassion for humanity, codependence is not. In codependency, you are a slave to other people's interests. In helping, you will learn that not all people you help will appreciate you. Some may even resent you. On the other hand, those who are perpetually recipient of your help may cause you to resent them. Both ways, resentment is destructive. Instead of giving up in a painful way in order to please, learn to give without causing pain. Learn to give while not sacrificing your own happiness. Though, this is not a ticket to selfishness which is just the opposite polarity.

16. Stop feeling personally responsible for others when you are not

We are responsible for the betterment of ourselves and our common being. However, there is a limit to how much we are responsible for others. We are not responsible for their mistakes and its consequences. You cannot be responsible for someone else happiness, no matter how much you try – instead, you will end up being unhappy. Thus, do not take the unnecessary burden of responsibility for someone else comfort and wellbeing. This conditions their mind to believe that they are helpless without you and are not capable of independence and responsibilities that come with it. You have to be like a teacher who knows when to help and when to withhold in order to teach a lesson.

Do not give help when you know that it is going to cause dependency on the other party. This is not helping. It is subjugation and control through psychological means.

17. Resist the urge to offer unsolicited advice

Most of the time, when you advise you inadvertently feel responsible for the consequences of your advice. It is good to advise as everyone needs it at one point or another. However, making it a habit of advising a particular person every now and then wears that person's mental self-reliance. Sometimes it is good to refuse to advise such a person in situations that you know are not dire such that whichever decision one makes will not have serious negative consequences but rather portends an opportunity to learn.

Self-learning is extremely important for one's independence, self-esteem, and growth. Unnecessary and unsolicited advice kills self-learning thus creating a conducive atmosphere for codependence.

18. Think before committing to something

Before committing yourself, ask yourself whether you are happy with the commitment or not. Seek to know whether you are doing it for your own good, to please the other party or for mutual benefit. Weigh the cost-benefit tradeoff. Does the commitment leave you better off or worse off? Does it contribute to you losing your space, independence and resolve? Does it dampen your willpower? What is the alternative to committing? What are the consequences of this alternative? Does committing level the playing field or does it tilt to unfair disadvantage? Does the commitment aim to trap either of the unwilling parties?

It is important that the commitment is intended for mutual gain, raising an equal platform, and out of free will. If it is not, then, the likely consequence is codependence.

Yet, commitments, though with the best of all intents never always yield positive results. Thus, it is important to clearly state what one expects as the outcome of such a commitment so that if the intended outcome is not achieved, then, there is freedom to exit from such a commitment.

19. Honor your needs

When it comes to engagement and making commitments, it is important that you honor your needs rather than sacrificing them so as to satisfy the other person's needs. Be honest of your own needs in any agreement or commitment. Do not suppress them out of fear of not pleasing the other party. Each party should know and should be capable of negotiating and exchanging the trade-offs. A strong mutual relationship is built on the foundation of making mutual sacrifices for optimal mutual gain.

Shying away from being honest with your needs will inadvertently lead to you being in a disadvantageous position. It may not necessarily mean being exploited by the other party but most likely lead to unknowingly being disadvantaged by the other party.

20.   Listen to your inner feelings

Your inner feelings are extremely intuitive. Do not suppress your discomfort, doubt, concern, opinion, judgment or feeling. Allow yourself time and space to understand them and evaluate them so that you can arrive at your own conclusions and make an informed decision.

Do not allow yourself to become subject to pressures of the urgency of the moment. If you feel there is undue pressure, that is a strong signal to back off.

21. When you are hurt, address the cause

Inevitably, there will be moments when you get hurt in any relationship. No human is perfect. Even with the best intentions, you may end up being hurt or hurting someone else. Thus, learning to accept that you are hurt and seek its root cause is important in addressing the hurt. Nonetheless, never leave any hurt to go unaddressed as this pile up to create a wound. The more the wound gets injured, the more the pain and the longer it will take to heal. Even after healing, the deeper and wider will be the scar.

Always be brave enough to exclaim your hurt. Be ready to communicate it to your partner in such a manner that brings understanding rather than conflict. Do not be quick to apportion blame unless you are certainly sure that the person hurting you is deliberate.

Importantly, sharpen your sensitivity to hurting by being conscious of your needs, wants, thoughts and feelings. Obviously, do not overdo it. But, neither should you suppress your sensitivity.

22.   Do not insult your partner

Resorting to insults, criticism and blame games harden positions. Worse of it is when you label them with demeaning words. These labels will never be forgotten. They help to poison a relationship and increase codependence as the abused, blamed and criticized partner feels inadequate.

23.   Find your way of handling conflicts

Learn to handle conflicts. Conflicts in a relationship will never cease to exist. Conflicts are healthy. They are a sign of diversity and alternative views. What is important is to manage them so that they become of benefit rather than pain to the relationship. Explore different modes of conflict resolution until you arrive at one that fits both parties. A conflict resolution that fits both of you will make you stronger and happier after every conflict.

## 24.	Work on developing yourself

Focusing on winning others' approval veers you off from your own path into their path. This means that you sacrifice your goals for their goals. When you stop pursuing your goals for their sake, you forfeit self-development.

You have to get back to your inner senses and explore your feelings, desires, and goals. Work towards setting your own goals and making own decisions to pursue them.

## 25.	Believe in yourself

One of the greatest weaknesses of codependence is lack of self-belief. Most codependents do not have faith in their own abilities and thus suspends them for the benefit of other people's abilities. It is due to lack of self-beliefs that make most of codependents to become subconsciously and instinctively seeking to play a second fiddle to other people's beliefs.

Take the personal effort to work on your own abilities and capabilities. Do not let mistakes discourage you for they are not problems but rather opportunities to learning better ways of doing things. Mistakes help you to know what works and what does not work.

Learn to accept who you are. Do not feel inadequate or sorry for your being. You lack nothing. You are inferior to no one. You are a not an imperfect being but simply a different being. All you need is to chart your own path. In your own path, there will be less desire for comparison and competition. You will trek confidently knowing that you are the first and only creator of your path.

26.   Keep a journal

A journal is an important tool, yet most people ignore it. Keep a journal that you can update every moment you need to update it. Do not labor to devise a formula for writing, as this will make you ignore those things that seem not to fit into it. Simply write what you observe, be it your thoughts, feelings, emotions, experiences, observations, etc. This way, you will be able to identify a pattern that probably leads to codependence and break it.

A journal will help you keep note of small stuff that you always ignore but which are tips of the iceberg in your relationship. They are like leaking drops of water that you ignore for their minute size only to realize later that the tank is empty.

27.   Lift your self–esteem and confidence

Self-esteem is about seeing yourself in a positive image. You can only see yourself positively if you deem yourself to be making achievements and attaining your goals. You feel positive when you are confident in your abilities and appreciate your personal attributes – be they strengths or weaknesses.

Free yourself from the vicious cycle of negative thoughts. Somehow, you cannot stop thoughts from flowing. But, you can stop your attachment to the thoughts. Mindfulness is one such practice that allows you to be an independent observer of your thoughts such that they do not affect you unless you deliberately choose to be affected by them.

28. Give without expecting anything in return

What hurts most of the caregivers in a codependent relationship is the hurt that comes with feeling unappreciated for the positive gesture. Like in any other relationships, when you give a gift, you should not expect anything in return. This frees you from the longings of appreciation. Do it because you want to share and free yourself from the burden of possessing. See it as a way of rendering your service to others. See it as an expression of love and compassion rather than a bribe for 'thank you'.

29. Be around people who are good for you

Humans are social beings, just as most animals are. This is the nature of being. Companionship is like a blanket or warm clothing in cold weather. With companionship, you can keep off from the biting cold of loneliness. Yet, it is a dry blanket that will give you warmth, not a wet one. Keep off from wet blankets. Wet blankets are those people who dwell in dampening your spirit, who sip away your energy and wear out your resolve. They are psychic vampires that find all the opportunities to devour your inner being and suck out your self-esteem. Keep off them.

Seek companionship with people who ignite embers of joy within you - people who make you forget negative thoughts and feelings, and people who encourage you and appreciate your being. These are people worth your social investment.

CHAPTER EIGHT: OVERCOMING LAZINESS, BECOMING MOTIVATED AND MORE PRODUCTIVE

Laziness is a condition that is as old as humankind. The consequences of laziness are proverbial. Yet, laziness is one of the subjects that have been taken for granted. It has become some sort of a normalized label which gets applied whenever someone's performance is unsatisfactory or below par. Does every underperformance or lack of it mean laziness? Well, we can tell this by having a proper perspective of what laziness means.

What is laziness?

Laziness is a mental condition in which the person lacks the willpower to overcome inertia with regard to the specific or general performance of duty. It is a condition characterized by avoidance of responsibility, which results into one not carrying out tasks that ought to be done or carrying them in such a manner that results into delays, poor quality outcomes, and general sub-optimality.

What drives people into laziness?

We have previously seen the root causes of addiction and codependence. We have seen how some of the symptoms of addiction and codependence are often treated as the real disease hence making it hard to find the real solution. Thus, it is important to understand what drives people into laziness so that we can distinguish the root causes from the symptoms.

The Eight Mental Voices of Laziness

As we have stated, laziness is a mental condition. Thus, it is not a disease in itself but a symptom resulting from one or several causes.

Laziness manifests itself in various facets of expression. The following are the most common of these voices of laziness:

1. Confusion: "I don't know what to do."

One of the leading causes of procrastination is confusion. When you do not know what to do, when to do it and sometimes even how to do it, then you will most likely delay taking action.

This means that in some sort of way, there is a mental block. Your mental power is overwhelmed in establishing a creative solution to the task/challenge at hand. More often than not, this could be as a result of not really understanding why you need to act since you are either overwhelmed by the seemingly gigantic task at hand or you do not appreciate that it is inevitable that you quickly swing into action. When there is lack of appreciation of the urgency and the importance of tackling the task at hand, procrastination sets in. Furthermore, if there are no serious consequences for not acting, then, it becomes less costly not to act.

Thus, confusion could be a signal to lack of fair understanding and appreciation of the task/challenge at hand.

2. Fixed Mindset: "I'm afraid I'll fail or look stupid."

A fixed mindset is a one that is not dynamic and adaptable to changing circumstances and thus is not ready to embrace new perspectives. Like being afraid of failure or looking stupid before others is a form of neurotic fear etched in the fixed mindset which is not ready to accept the possibility of succeeding and not being considered 'stupid' after all, whether succeeding or not. It is a mindset that does not want to appreciate that attempting is a success in itself despite the eventual outcome and that learning is a process that begins by taking the first initiative.

3. Lethargy: "I'm too tired. I don't have the energy."

Lethargy happens due to chronic fatigue. It is a product of low energy. It is mostly due to being over-active and thus spending energy faster than it is being replenished. The brain reacts by directing the body to resist temptations to work more, especially the same activity that causes it to expend more energy than it is ready to replenish.

The best way to deal with lethargy is to accept that we are fatigued. This means we need to find the best way to rest. It could be taking a nap, switching to a less energy-consuming activity for a break (job rotation), relaxing (taking annual leave), engaging in activities that help to remove body stresses and strains such as yoga, massage, spa, etc. You can also engage in brain relaxation exercises such as meditation, Zhan Zhuang, or grounding exercises.

There are always temptations to using stimulants such as coffee, marijuana, among others when you feel lethargic. This only helps to entrench the vicious cycle with the risk of causing addiction while not addressing the root cause. With lethargy, laziness sets it.

4. Apathy: "I just don't care about anything."

Apathy is a strong message that depression is knocking. Apathy creeps in when we are disharmonious with our greater calling or purpose in life. When we are doing things that run contrary to our goals, our passions, our calling, or our core interests, then our mind reacts in such a way to switch off from continuing with such things. Thus, we start developing disinterest or apathy towards such engagements.

The most important thing you need to do in order to stop apathy is to carry out an audit of what you are doing and whether that aligns with your greatest aspirations. If you find that what you are doing is not in line with or does not help to further your aspiration, then, it is important that you redraw your path. Alternatively, you could be doing the right thing, but you are stuck to the old goals that ceased to be relevant. That means you must rediscover your core values and repurpose your goals so that you can have an inspiring vision.

Apathy is simply lack of inspiration. With perpetual apathy, laziness sets in.

5. Regret: "I'm too old to get started. It's too late."

Regrets are as a result of dwelling on the negative past experiences as a reference to our present. It is a mindset problem. While it is important to learn lessons so that we do not repeat the same experience, it is also important not to dwell on the painful part of the experience. However painful the experience is, let us consign its pain to where it belongs – the past. We must be able to grieve enough of our pain so that when we move on, we are less attached to the pain.

The worst regrets are for things left undone. This is when you start regretting "how I wish I did it. But, I am too old to get started. It is too late". It is never too late unless it is not worth it. If it is still worth it, you must do it, right now. If it is not worth it, do not regret that "it is too late" for the problem is not the time but its worthlessness. That which is not worthy has no value to keep thinking about it.

6. Identity: "I'm just a lazy person."

This is negative self-labeling. Every time you label yourself negatively, you reinforce that negative perception of yourself. This grants you an excuse to fit into your self-label. Instead, we need to have an inquisitive mindset that seeks to find solutions to our weaknesses rather than surrendering to them in the form of negative self-labeling.

Whenever you find yourself attempting to utter such negative self-label, quickly remind yourself that this is a mask you are trying to hide in to avoid the responsibility required to confront your laziness. Snap out of it. Keep finding your stronger points and focus on building them rather than surrendering to the weaker points. We are lazy by not discovering our strengths.

7. Shame: "I shouldn't be so lazy."

Shame, just like negative self-labeling (negative identity), is a mask you hide in to avoid your consciousness. Address your nakedness and dress it properly rather than running to hide. You will never take a free walk with others in pursuit of livelihood if you have to hide away from the course.

8. Neurotic Fear: "I just can't."

Neurotic fear is not that which occurs when you encounter physical danger such that you have to either take a fight or flight. Neurotic fear is internally generated and only needs an external trigger to happen. It is etched in our mindset, mostly due to our past traumatic experiences. Thus, whenever there is an external trigger the mind compares it to the past trauma and hence instructs the brain to generate a learned response of what ought to be done when such a scenario happens.

To be able to deal with neurotic fear, you must snap out of the fixed mindset and embrace different possibilities and opportunities. It is to accept that neurotic fear is about an entrenched position (ego) that you do not want to risk losing. Thus, you must first accept that there is ego that you do not want to get bruised. Once you realize that it is actually an ego problem, then, it will be much easier to deal with the ego itself (the root cause) rather than its symptom (fear).

You must identify your neurotic needs and the neurotic patterns/habits that you have engendered to address them. It is only by doing these that you can be able to address your neuroticism that is responsible for your neurotic fear.

The key drivers of laziness

The key drivers of laziness include poor mindset, fear, lack of motivation, lack of willpower, distraction, low energy, procrastination, and poor lifestyle.

Poor mindset

It all begins in the mind. It too can end in the mind. You are endowed with immense ability to rewire and reset your mindset. You have no reason whatsoever to remain stuck with a poor mindset – a mindset that limits you, distorts your perception of reality and hinders you from creating your desired reality. If you cannot get it, make it. Yes, this can seem obnoxious, but it works in most of the cases.

All the other drivers of your laziness derive their blueprint from your poor mindset. Your poor mindset is the ground from which their roots are established.

Fear

As we have seen from the 8 faces of laziness that neurotic fear can result into laziness. For example, when you imagine how you worked hard to perform a certain task only for your client to refuse to pay or terminate the work midway by telling you that you lacked sufficient skills, or your work was of poor quality, you are more likely to develop neurotic fear when you are brought such tasks in future. In this case, it is your past pain that you are using to subconsciously decline performance. All you need is to realize that not all clients are like him/her. Even if it were true that you had inadequate skills, that should not stop you from further learning and enhancing your skills.

A fixed mindset will treat your negative experience as a stumbling block to performance. A growth mindset will treat a negative experience as an opportunity to learn new ways of doing things. You have to reset your mindset from a fixed one to a growth one if you have to overcome your neurotic fear.

Lack of motivation

Lethargy and apathy are products of lack of motivation. Motivation is a positive attitude towards a given performance. When you lack motivation towards the performance of a given task, then you will find yourself being lethargic or apathetic towards it.

Lack of motivation occurs due to poor attitude, which itself could be caused by negative beliefs. For example, when you believe that a certain task is demeaning of your caliber, is not for your gender or age, or is beyond your capacity to perform, you are more likely going to avoid it. Thus, with no alternative task to perform, you end up being idle. When this becomes habitual, you find yourself being perpetually lazy such that when you are eventually faced with those tasks you deem positive, you end up not performing them because you have conditioned your body to comfort itself in idleness.

Low energy

You require energy in order to make effort. Without energy, no effort. Without effort, no work is done. Energy is not just the physical energy. Mental energy is also extremely important. In fact, it is the mental energy that controls how, when, where, why, and what kind of physical energy needs to be expended towards a given task. It is the mental energy that drives the thought process required for planning and execution. There are some tasks that require more mental energy than physical energy such as professional office tasks. On the other hand, there are those that require more physical energy than mental energy such as fieldwork (such as gardening, mining, extraction, construction, among others) or factory work (such as production, assembly, fabrication, etc).

Lethargy is one of the symptoms of low energy – both mental and physical. Lethargy is mostly due to mismanagement of your energy resources due to poor planning. Thus, having a planning mindset can help you keep off lethargy.

Lack of willpower

Lack of willpower is a combination of low mental energy accompanied with lack of motivation. This means that you lack sufficient inner drive to overcome inertia. This creates a mental resistance towards expending your energy (effort) in carrying out a given task. Willpower is a mental muscle. Like a physical muscle, you need to exercise it often for it to strengthen, be in good form and provide optimal output. Motivation is the ignition key that lights up the willpower which drives one to achieve set objectives and goals.

To overcome inertia, you need to craft the right mindset that brings forth a positive attitude towards waking up to challenges. Thus, challenges should make you wake up instead of making you sleep off. Whether you will wake up to confront challenge or sleep off to avoid it depends solely on your attitude. It is your attitude that serves as the ignition of your willpower.

Distraction

Distraction is an element of lack of planning mindset. A planning mindset has an in-built self-discipline mechanism. Without self-discipline, you easily become distracted and follow the waves of the moment just like a flag following the wind.

Distraction can be in the form of people, environmental noise, electronic gadgets, among others. Most of the distractions can be avoided by having strict appointment discipline. Even environmental noise can be reduced by relocating or redesigning your house/office interiors.

The worst thing you can do is to invite distraction through habitual addiction. If you are addicted to distractions such as social media, playing games, online gambling, among others, then you have an extremely serious problem.

Procrastination

Procrastination is characterized by lack of willpower and inertia. Lack of motivation and fear are the two primary causes of procrastination. Fear could include fear of success, fear of failure, fear of expectations, and fear of consequences.

Fear of failure - happens when we feel inadequate and thus afraid of negative outcomes (underperformance or poor results).

Fear of success - happens when we feel that if we become successful we are likely going to be punished. For example, this 'punishment' may take the form of being given higher and more challenging responsibilities, upsetting our partners such that they become jealous and thus straining or ending the relationship, fear of being praised and being exposed to publicity (more so, for introverts).

Fear of expectations - happens when one sets a low standard of performance just to avoid expectations that come with higher performance.

Fear of consequences - happens when one perceives negative consequences of a successful performance. This can be a situation where there is a weak leadership that fears being challenged. For example, creative artists and journalists may fear to achieve their highest level of creativity as this could be interpreted as a criticism to the powers-that-be. Cartoonists, poets, literal writers, journalists have all faced serious punishment and even death for simply expressing their creativity.

The desire for nurture - can also breed procrastination, which results in laziness. This happens mostly with younger siblings in a family who want to be nurtured by their parents or older siblings. They will deliberately fail to perform or poorly perform certain tasks so that the tasks are taken over by their parents or elder siblings. For example, a person may deliberately iron slowly or be slow in making breakfast just to force the older sibling or parent to take over the task in order to avoid lateness. When this becomes a habit, it breeds laziness.

Passive-aggressive communication - occurs whereby one party withdraws services either deliberately or subconsciously as a way of expressing dissatisfaction while avoiding conflict. For example, a wife can start to habitually delay making dinner resulting in her husband either doing it or occasionally sleeping hungry. On the other hand, a dissatisfied husband may start to habitually come home late and avoid intimacy as an expression of dissatisfaction with his wife.

Mental disease – sometimes procrastination may not be deliberate. It can be as a result of a mental disease. For example, many depressed people are prone to procrastination and indecisiveness. They may find themselves mentally stuck and rather than taking action, they resort to self-loathing and procrastination.

Poor lifestyle

Poor lifestyle can contribute to both low mental and physical energy. The following are some of the contributors to poor lifestyle:

- Poor nutrition – poor nutrition could be either a result of not eating enough food or eating enough food but of poor quality. It can also be a result of overeating. For example, poor nutrition can trigger stress hormones thus resulting in low mental energy. Also, certain nutritional deficiencies can result in low brain power. On the other hand, not eating enough or eating a diet that lacks sufficient carbohydrates can result in low physical energy. Overeating and bingeing can result in obesity. Obesity is one of the leading causes of stress and depression, among other conditions.

- Sedentary lifestyle - a lifestyle characterized by low physical activity levels. Our modern lifestyle is by default a sedentary lifestyle. We spend a lot of our time studying, sitting in offices or standing in factory floors. When we are going to work/study or heading back home, we are either driving or being driven. Thus, we lack sufficient physical mobility. Without deliberate interventions to carry out physical fitness exercises, our mind is tuned towards the lesser physical effort, which means that we develop inertia towards physical activities.

Effort-motivation imbalance

Effort-motivation balance determines whether one pursues a goal or not. One can only pursue a goal if their level of motivation matches the effort necessary to achieve the goal. Laziness is a situation whereby one is not motivated enough to expend the required effort to achieve their goal.

Can addiction and codependence cause laziness?

There is a correlation between laziness and addiction or codependence. However, not all lazy people are addicts and not all addicts are necessarily lazy. But, in some cases, it happens – depending on the type of addiction. A significant number of substance addicts become lazy and codependent. Nonetheless, it is hard to tell what causes the other, between laziness and codependence (Taker). Codependence (Taker) can make one become lazy and also laziness can make one become a Taker.

How to overcome laziness

Overcoming laziness means gaining the ability to do things that we want to do. It means becoming successful. Success is about accomplishing milestones involving a few big things and a lot of small things. It is about doing those important yet unpleasant things that we feel inclined to avoid. The key difference between success and failure is how one blends the performance of big things with the small things.

The Secret Key to Overcoming Laziness

You can overcome your laziness. Those people who are highly productive were never born productive. They chose to become productive. Though environment and upbringing can influence your productivity while growing up, as an adult you make your own choices. One of these choices is overcoming your past and changing your course. Thus, as an adult, there should be no excuses about your past that make you stick to laziness and encourage lack of productivity.

Nonetheless, let us focus on the key secrets to overcoming laziness:

1. Determine if you are really lazy, or just overwhelmed

Being busy and being lazy are two opposite polarities, none of them being healthy to our wellbeing. As we have seen, laziness can be a consequence of unrelenting busyness that allows lethargy and apathy to set in. Thus, if you are overwhelmed by a busy schedule, you may end up feeling 'lazy'. Yet, if you think that you need to do more to overcome this 'laziness' you may end up taking extra-measures such as the use of stimulants to force your already tired and overwhelmed body to do more. This may cause other challenges such as stress and depression resulting into painful experiences (such as headaches) that may lead to vicious abuse of other substances such as depressants.

Thus, stepping back to determine whether you are really lazy or just overwhelmed is important. Otherwise, you may end up taking actions that further the disease by attempting to heal the symptom rather than confronting its root causes.

2. Figure out the real issue (root cause)

Like every other unhealthy condition, you need to carry out an appropriate diagnosis of the real issue or root cause behind your laziness.

Irrespective of the various root causes, you can break down your problem into the following three key issues:

- **Lack of self-discipline** – lack of self-discipline can affect a whole lot of things. It can affect your goals, it can cause distractions, it can make your plans fail, it can cause inefficiency and ineffective utilization of your time, effort and resources, among others.

- **Unrealistic expectations** – it is important to base your expectations on SMART goals. SMART goals are Specific, Measurable, Attainable, Realistic and Timely. Let SMART goals be part of your overall planning. Unrealistic expectations set in when we take up tasks that are overwhelming to our abilities (skills, energy, effort) and resources (time and factors of production). For your expectations to be realistic, they must not override your need for rest, relaxation, social and emotional connections, and leisure.

- **Lack of motivation** – motivation is the inner drive towards accomplishing your goals. Lack of self-discipline and unrealistic expectations can contribute to lack of motivation. Other factors that can contribute to lack of motivation include your habits, attitudes, beliefs, and fears. All these are part of your mindset. You need to change your mindset in order to overcome bad habits, poor attitude, negative beliefs, and fears.

3. Change your mindset

There is a lot about the mindset that we cannot fully explore in this book. However, we can narrow down to the following core elements that you need to deal with in order to change your mindset:

- Reframe your thinking – practice positive thinking. You can use techniques such as neuroplasticity and neuro-linguistic programming to change your thought patterns.
- Disrupt your old habitual patterns – every habit has three core elements; trigger, routine and reward. You must overcome your trigger, disrupt the routine and substitute the reward with better reward under new habits.
- Make new habits – create habits that help to reinforce the achievement of your goals.
- Create behavior chains that reinforce the new habits – habits become entrenched in your mindset every time they get repeated. Behaviors are simply actions that you take, and all attributes associated with taking the action. One technique that can enable you to create behavior chains that reinforce your new habits is Habit Stacking.

- Monitor your self-talk — instead of negative self-talk, engage in positive affirmation.

- Practice mindfulness — mindfulness is about being self-aware. You need to consciously and deliberately practice awareness of your thought process, thought patterns and thought output.

- Engender a planning mindset — a planning mindset is one that flexibly adjusts to plans. Plans are never fixed but adjustable to changing circumstances. A fixed mindset is one that fails to adjust to changing plans. Lethargy, apathy and loss of motivation are more often a result of a fixed mindset that has failed to adjust to changing circumstances. Planning is part of organizing. Thus, you need to organize your environment to be able to effectively plan.

4. Focus on the actual problem.

After figuring out the real issue and resetting your mind, the next crucial step is to focus on the actual problem. Organize yourself around dealing with the problem. Visualize your goals and set a mission to achieve them. Derive plans based on your vision, mission, and goals. While there may be small urgent things that you need to handle immediately to snap out of your laziness, stopping laziness requires a long-term approach.

5. Think of the benefits of not being lazy

One way to get motivated to sit down and plan your life is to think of the benefits of not being lazy. Look at what you would have achieved had you not been lazy. Think about what you are likely going to achieve by altering your course away from laziness. This could be the course that you never felt energized to study, the project that you kept-off for long (such as developing an app), going on an adventurous trip to discover new environments, among others.

It is by thinking about the future benefits that you can develop a vision that allows you to rise above obstacles of the current circumstances.

6. Thinking about the consequences

The other way to motivate yourself into planning your next course of action is to think about the consequences of you staying lazy. The current consequences will help you fathom the depth of your laziness. This could be the low-paying job simply because you were too lazy to learn better skills; closed business simply because you were too lazy to keep a daily wake-up routine or too lazy to go the extra mile to serve your customers better or too lazy to explore other sources of income to sustain it. There are many such consequences. Most of us have been lazy at one point in time and thus can easily relate to the consequences.

More importantly, focus on the future. Think about the likely future consequences should you not stop being lazy. This could mean not taking your children to better schools thus making them suffer the consequences of your laziness, not affording a good home, among others.

Thinking about the consequences helps you appreciate the 'punishment' you are likely going to suffer should you not snap out of your lazy habits.

7. Get organized

Getting organized simply means that you become purpose-driven. Instead of letting situations and circumstances dictate you, you dictate them. The following are the things that you must start with:

- **Un-clutter your life** – clutters are things that obscure your vision and distract your attention. They could be physical (environmental), mental, or social. Start with your physical environment. Get rid of unnecessary stuff from your house and office. Arrange your house and office by keeping everything in order. Remove unnecessary distractions from within your reach such as TV, game consoles, social media notifications, etc. The next thing to un-clutter is your thought. Keep off negative thoughts by resetting your mindset. The third thing you need to un-clutter is your relationships (social circles). Keep off people who distract you. Keep off those people who are always calling you during working hours to talk about personal things. Keep off those people who are always urging you to indulge in addictive behaviors.

- **Keep a record** – have a to-do list, notebook, and journal. The to-do list will remind you and guide you on the tasks that you need to perform and accomplish. The notebook will help you capture your ideas, observations, and perceptions. You can use a journal to record your daily encounters related to your work and activities.

- **Start with the unpleasant tasks** – if there are those tasks that you would rather avoid but have to do, the best way to deal with them is when your mental and physical energy are collectively at the apex – in the morning. Start with those unpleasant tasks. This will not only strengthen your willpower but will also help you to be motivated to do more as you will feel like you have conquered the day early enough.

- **Delegate** – If the source of your laziness is lethargy. Then, it simply means you are overwhelmed and exhausted. Delegating is the best way to stop being overwhelmed. Find those mundane tasks that do not require your creative thinking and find someone else to do them for you. Think about those around you. Find out how you can utilize them in helping you carry these mundane tasks. This could be your friend, spouse, child, coworker, partner, personal assistant, virtual assistant or any other person that can offer a helping hand.

- **Keep time** – You must remain ever vigilant and conscious of time. Time is limited. Your performance is against time. Your income and costs are based on time.

- **Take advantage of organizers** – organizers are tools that help you to organize yourself or keep organized. These include a checklist, timetable, calendar, diary, Gantt charts, Network diagrams, among others.

8. Plan

If you fail to plan, then you have planned to fail. This is an old adage yet remains so true. While some plans do fail, do not forget that nothing succeeds without a plan.

- Have a vision – of who and what you want to be. Make it a habit to reflect on the life you want to live, the goals you want to achieve and the person you want to be.

- Establish your mission – have a purpose-driven life anchored on the reason for your existence and reason for wanting to accomplish your vision.

- Set SMARTEST goals – Set goals that are not only Specific, Measurable, Achievable, Realistic, and Timely (SMART), but also Empowering, Stimulating, and Transformational (EST).
- Have a strategy (plan of action) – a plan of action is a step-by-step plan on how you are going to implement your mission to achieve your goal and enliven your vision.

9. Implement your plan of action

Implementation is putting your plan of action into practice. It is actualizing it based on specific objectives aimed at achieving your goals. Each objective must target a certain goal or part of it (stage, milestone, task, process, etc). Lay out tactics (with appropriate techniques) that will guide your operations.

The following are tactics necessary to implement your plan of action:

- Break your work into small manageable tasks
- Lay out how you are going to implement the tasks in terms of scheduling (e.g. which task comes first, and which one follows next). You can use Gantt charts and network diagrams.
- Set objectives for each task
- Set target (milestone) for each objective

- Map out processes, resources, skills and techniques required to achieve your target and acquire them
- Set a control mechanism for your implementation process – a control mechanism is one that allows you to set expected standards, measure performance, and take corrective measures should the actual result deviate from the expected result (standard).
- Carry out your implementation

Tips to succeed:

i. Start with just a small step forward.
ii. Do a small part of what matters most at your most optimal time (first thing in your day).
iii. Do one thing at a time (focus management).
iv. Take your time.
v. Ask for help when you need it.
vi. Be self-disciplined.
vii. Compliment yourself every for every little progress you make.
viii. Shut down the escape routes (distractions) temporarily.
ix. Stay on track.
x. Do not give up.
xi. Do not compromise on your rest, sleep and exercise
xii. Make sure you are not overwhelmed.
xiii. Measure the changes (in the new habits).

xiv. Look for alternatives (to avoid overworking e.g. streamlining the process, automation, outsourcing, delegation, etc).

xv. Remember, nothing changes until you do.

xvi. Appreciate your work.

xvii. Appreciate your time.

xviii. Appreciate your progress.

10. Reward your success

It is always good to reward your success. Rewards trigger a part of the brain responsible for the 'feel good' effect. This, in turn, raises your self-motivation and desires to do more in order to experience the same 'good effect' even more. This is the best way to acquire the habit of success.

11. Enjoy your rest, sleep and leisure

Rest is the way to allow your body to rejuvenate. Sleeping is akin to taking your body to the garage for repairs and maintenance. Most of us are quick to take our vehicles to the garage than our bodies. The result is wreckage and lethargy. Find ways to enjoy your rest, sleep and leisure. This way, your brain will always be quick to switch you to that state requiring rest, sleep and leisure.

Staying Motivated

It is easier to become motivated than to stay motivated. To stay motivated is to perpetually remain in that state of motivation. To achieve this, you need to:

1) Practice creative visualization – visualization is very powerful in entrenching your thoughts. Visualize doing those tasks that you plan to do in an enthusiastic and energetic way. Visualize yourself accomplishing the task and celebrating the outcome.

2) Make a checklist of the desires, goals, and motivations you want to move towards – going through a checklist of your desires, goals, and motivations on a frequent basis helps you not only gain a better perspective of them but also refine them further. This way, you are able to come up with a much better approach to dealing with your tasks.

3) Regularly revisit the importance and value of your goals – reminding yourself of the importance of your goals and the value that you are going to gain from achieving them. This helps to reinforce your resolve and thus strengthen your willpower.

4) Tell yourself you can do it – Reminding yourself that you can do it helps to create that self-confidence and raise

self-esteem. Use a record of your achievements and of those who achieved similar task to build this confidence.

5) Realize that life is about trading costs and benefits – there are those moments you may ask yourself "is it worth the cost?" when things get tough. This is probably because you are reflecting on what you have sacrificed to be where you are and subconsciously feel that it is not worth it. Just remind yourself that there is no gain without sacrifice. You had to exactly sacrifice what you have done in order to attain the current progress. There will always be cost-benefit tradeoffs. Do not be scared when your mind comes to such an evaluation. It is healthy. But, remember not to give up.

6) Be gracious in your steps – do not overwhelm yourself by forcing giant steps that will tire you soon. This is not a sprint but marathon.

7) Share your goals – sometimes being accountable only to yourself is not motivating enough. Share your goals with your loved ones. They will keep prompting you about your progress. This will make you feel convicted to perform. Above all, they will inspire you when you are low and be able to help you out where they can.

8) Taking it normal when stumbling from time to time. There is a reason why the ground not always flat. The

landscape is more beautiful when there are hills and valleys.

9) Tap into the energy, enthusiasm, and motivation of others

10) Practice positive thinking and positive affirmations

11) Take lessons from those who have been from where you are before you

12) Be kind to yourself – do not hurt yourself, be it physically, mentally, psychologically, socially, or emotionally simply because you have to achieve success. That is not the essence of it all. The ultimate essence is to achieve your greater being – neither laziness nor work-slavery.

We can now revisit how Edgar and Maria faired on. Though both Edgar and Maria had some early childhood experiences that made them become such irresponsible and lazy, counseling lessons did help them snap out.

Edgar discovered his talent as a gym instructor. He also tried his hands at tattooing and found that he was a good artist. Working as an artist and gym instructor earned him enough. He later found a partner and married. The partner is a nurse. They became a great combination. He became more productive and supportive of his partner. They married, bought a home and have a successful family with two children.

Maria, though she loved cosmetics and matters to deal with beauty, her talent was not in that field. However, she found herself marketing beauty related products on behalf of the various beauty companies. She became highly successful. She kept her frame fit, with the help of her brother at the gym. She also added health and wellness products to her line of products that she marketed. She was able to overcome her past addiction and become a successful marketer. She has great plans of launching her own private label and has already met most of the requirements.

Both Edgar and Maria found a purpose and meaning to their lives. The learned lessons the hardest of ways and decided to stop and turn to a new chapter of renewed vigor, purpose and achievement.

Not only did they manage to banish addiction, codependence, and laziness from their lives, they were able to reconnect their broken bonds with their respective loved ones, strengthen them, and be there for them. The fruits of their productivity flourished, and they enjoyed the happiness that comes with achieving one's goals and being cherished by loved ones.

Addiction, laziness and codependence can be overcome.

CONCLUSION

Thank you for acquiring this book and reading it up to this point.

This book provides practical information on how to overcome addiction, codependence, and laziness. I hope you can use the information provided in this book to help yourself, a loved one, friend, peer, colleague or neighbor who is suffering from addiction, codependence, or laziness to overcome it. It is also my sincere hope that you have been inspired enough to recommend this book to those who need it so that they too can embark on a journey to recovery.

Again, thank you for acquiring this book.

Good luck!

Made in the USA
Las Vegas, NV
17 July 2023